To Lourri,

Best wishes

Michael

THE BISHOP WEARS NO DRAWERS

A Former Catholic Missionary Priest Remembers Africa

MICHAEL BARRINGTON

ISBN: 978-1-4834-3225-0 (sc)
ISBN: 978-1-4834-3227-4 (hc)
ISBN: 978-1-4834-3226-7 (e)

Library of Congress Control Number: 2015908556

Lulu Publishing Services rev. date: 08/06/2015

For my wife:
my best friend,
my lover,
my soul mate

PROLOGUE

"Mary, it's a boy, and he will be the next priest in the family!" I never actually heard these words spoken, since they were addressed by my grandmother to my mother just a few moments after she delivered me. They would, however, establish a family expectation and set off a chain of events that would predictably lead to my eventual ordination.

The most influential person in my life, next to my mother, was 'Jas' Simpson. At least that's what everybody called him. His correct title, of course, was the Reverend Father James Simpson, a Catholic priest and a Holy Ghost Father. Both he and my uncle went through the seminary together and were ordained on the same day. I remember him sitting around our kitchen table playing cards with my parents and uncle, sleeves rolled up, wearing red suspenders, and drinking whiskey. Most of the time, they spent laughing as Jas spun one tale after another. I was probably ten years old at the time, and had been looking forward to his visit for days. My family frequently spoke about what a wonderful priest Jas was, but above all, they said that he was on furlough after spending five years in Africa, and would be showing us his photos.

Larger than life, a non-stop joker, and not averse to using profanities, he threw off his jacket and Roman collar almost as soon as he entered the house. My Catholic altar-boy sensibilities were both shocked and excited. I had no idea that this kind of priest existed. The time he spent with my four sisters and me showing us his photos felt very special: we saw pictures of people with tribal markings on their faces and intricate braided hair, of mud huts with grass roofs, strange flowers and animals, and even one of Jas himself in a dug-out canoe. He told us stories of poor children in Nigeria, explaining that this is where the pennies we collected at school for the 'foreign missions' were used. We were mesmerized. He allowed me to select one photo for myself as a gift, which I still have after all these years. I was hooked. I decided there and then that this is what I wanted to do with my life. I wanted to be just like Jas, to help the poor people of Africa.

Sixteen years later, I landed in Lagos, Nigeria, a newly ordained missionary priest, a Holy Ghost Father full of zeal, and with the highest of ideals. However, whether it was serendipity, chance, or divine intervention, my arrival took place at a pivotal moment both in the history of the Catholic Church and the political growth of Nigeria

For the Catholic Church, the years 1965-75 were of critical and momentous importance. The Second Vatican Council convened in Rome is considered to be the most significant religious event since the Reformation of the sixteenth century, and certainly the most important of the twentieth.

I was part of the new emergent theology that taught priests they were no longer leading a spiritual army bound for salvation, but were part of a pilgrim people striving for holiness. From the Bronx to Buenos Aires, London to Lagos, priests were now instructed to celebrate mass facing their congregations, communion rails were removed, and women no longer were obliged to cover their heads. Priests began fighting for integration and school decentralization, building housing for the poor, and speaking out on issues like nuclear disarmament and the Vietnam War. Birth control and abortion became open, contentious topics of discussion.

Convents opened their doors to the modern world, to the poor and to new mission opportunities. The traditional dress of religious nuns gave way to skirts, slacks, and jeans. Veils were shortened or abandoned. Priests and nuns began evaluating their vocations, and a new phenomenon took place, an exodus. Many left their ministry in order to get married. In the space of ten years, twenty-five thousand priests left the priesthood, and between 1996 and 2014 the number of priests in the USA had dropped by almost 45 percent. The Jesuits, the largest order of priests in the Church numbered almost 35,000 priests worldwide in 1996; in 2013 there were just over 17,000. The number of nuns who provided the backbone of Catholic education and health systems in the USA, dropped from 180,000 in 1966 to less than 50,000 in 2014 with an average age of 68.

All of this upheaval created tension and conflict throughout the Church, and especially in the mission fields, where the tradition of the "old" clashed head on with the liberating methods of the "new." Newly ordained missionaries like me were instructed to "Africanize" Christian living, and integrate into it the values of the local culture, in harmony with the Gospel. Emphasis was placed on providing religious services in the languages of the people, instead of the traditional Latin or English, and on developing a native clergy.

The Church today is still reeling from the recent revelation of countless notorious sexual scandals at even the highest levels of power. They have rocked the very foundations of what for decades presented itself as a stable, truthful, and respected Catholic society. Paradoxically, throughout Europe and North America many parishes are aging, attendances are dwindling, and churches are being closed, even while the number of people who actually call themselves Catholic is increasing. Churches in Africa and other developing countries, however, are exploding with worshippers served by the ever-increasing numbers of native clergy. The Diocese of Makurdi where I lived and worked with about sixty priests and nuns for ten years, is now divided into three separate jurisdictions with more than four hundred clergy, and all but a small handful are Nigerians.

I first arrived in Nigeria just as the country was tearing itself apart politically in a bloody civil war. It caused 100,000 military casualties, but between 500,000 and one million Biafran civilians died of starvation. The military would stay in power for the next eighteen years.

Situated on the northern edge of the war zone, Makurdi diocese was a major hub for the massing and deployment of troops. Movement for missionaries was severely restricted, making it difficult for them to minister to their huge sprawling parishes, since all roads into towns were usually guarded by two separate check points: one manned with armed, poorly trained military, and the other by the more experienced Nigerian Police. Essential supplies of every kind such as spare parts for trucks, gas, and canned goods were extremely limited, and access to local medical and dental care was virtually nonexistent. None of the missions had a telephone or short-wave radio, and the normal means of communication was either by word of mouth or hand carried letters. In the whole of this 50,000 square-mile diocese, there was only one narrow and pot-holed, paved, main road in such a state of disrepair that it was frequently closed during the monsoon season.

The Diocese of Makurdi, to which I had been assigned, had been without a bishop for almost three years. The only priests working there were white, mainly from England and Ireland, and with bitter, deep political differences that resulted in a repeated voting deadlock, and the inability to nominate a majority candidate. Rome finally intervened by selecting one of the nominees, and appointing a person who would quickly become a forward-thinking and progressive-minded bishop. Although that action would ultimately be pivotal for the dramatic growth and rapid development of the diocese, it did little to resolve the internal conflicts. It also seriously, negatively, and irrevocably affected the lives of many priests.

Some older priests, out of touch with the new theology, were unexpectedly removed from central, important, and well established parishes and appointed to remote mission stations in the bush. Sadly, others who were unable to cope with the changes and made to feel that they did not have a role to play in this new and rejuvenated Church, after a lifetime of dedicated ministry, simply left the country. They returned to England and Ireland where many, never having ministered to predominantly "white" congregations, failed to fit in, and experienced an even deeper sense of real alienation from their religious orders and the changing Church. They ended their days as lonely, estranged men and women.

"The Bishop Wears No Drawers" is the story of a young man's journey into this jungle of complexities: one he could never have imagined when he first set out with an idealistic vision of serving God and humanity in Africa.

CHAPTER 1

Politics

At first, it seemed like fun being squeezed with four other people into the noisy, shaking cab of this dilapidated wagon reeking of hot engine oil, as it lurched, creaked, and groaned its noisy way along the narrow, deep-rutted jungle paths. With more sacks being added at each stop there were more passengers, and as the loads got higher and higher I was concerned that the truck could overturn. My biggest concern, however, was the amount of time it was taking. After starting out in mid-morning, it was now late afternoon, and I was really worried about crossing through the military checkpoints in the dark.

With two flat tires on my Land Rover and no means of repairing them, I was stranded. The closest mechanic was in Otrukpo, forty-five miles away, and the only means of transport was by an all purpose ten ton truck, locally called a 'mammy wagon'. The following day was our local market, and I'd learned that several of these trucks would be coming into town with supplies. They would visit small hamlets on the way back, collecting sacks of rice for milling in Otrukpo, and of course, also collecting paying passengers. So I'd hitched a ride, along with my tires.

Even before we reached the main checkpoint, the driver had slowed the wagon down almost to a crawl, and rounding a bend we could hear soldiers shouting. The headlights from the truck created phantasmic shapes on the trees, accentuating the deep blackness that enveloped us. Then suddenly we arrived at the barrier: double strands of coiled barbwire stretched across the road, fastened at one end to a post. Off to the side, a drowsy looking soldier with an automatic weapon had been lounging on a bed of upturned ammunition boxes, but now he was caught in the headlights and was holding onto a rope attached to the wire. Our arrival had clearly disturbed his sleep.

As we slowly rolled to a stop, I noticed that ours was the only vehicle to be checked. Out of the darkness, a small group of soldiers quickly materialized: one waving a small flashlight, the others brandishing automatic weapons and holding bottles of Star beer in their hands. They shouted in a language I couldn't understand, other than the word "stop" many times. We were actually stopped, but this didn't appear to satisfy them.

"Who are you and what are you doing here at this late time?" A sweaty, black face with heavily blood-shot eyes had appeared at the driver's side and was peering into the cab. He was speaking in heavily-accented English.

"Get out. Get out," he bellowed. "Come with me."

Before the driver could comply, two other soldiers suddenly appeared out of the darkness and dragged him from his seat. A solitary, small kerosene bush lamp hanging on a forked stick in the clearing gave off an eerie, flickering, orange glow, and I could make out that they were having an animated discussion in front of a crude shack made out of old corrugated iron sheets. The three of us remaining in the cab just sat there in silence. There was no sound from any of the passengers perched high up on the sacks behind us. I was petrified.

Minutes later, they returned without the driver.

I wondered if he had not offered them a big enough bribe, a "dash," and if they were about to rob us.

"Which one of you has raped one of our women? We were told that it is somebody on this mammy wagon." A heavyset soldier with a couple of days growth on his chin, wearing a crumpled, dirty, and washed-out camouflage jacket that seemed several sizes too big was shouting into the cab.

He was clearly very drunk, and his pungent fetid breath reached even to where I was sitting. His statement made no sense to me at all.

Nobody moved.

"Get down, get down!" screamed a tall skinny soldier behind him. "Everybody get down now," all the while brandishing his weapon. "Where is that bad man?"

We all quickly stumbled down, keeping in the shadows next to the wagon as if somehow this would give us some protection. The passengers huddled in a group towards the rear. I was still convinced that all they wanted was our money.

Suddenly out of the shadows, an officer approached; at least he appeared to be in charge, since the other soldiers deferred to him.

In quite good English, but with a distinct slur, he announced, "If nobody will own up to this bad thing, then you will all be shot."

I could not believe my ears. But still nobody moved or spoke.

The officer then stormed off towards the shack, all the while saying something to his men. Two of them went inside, came out with what looked like a machine gun on a tripod, and set it up twenty yards directly in front of us.

"Line up, line up on this side," one of them shouted. It was parroted by several others. "Line up, line up now."

It was only at this point that I realized they were deadly serious. Here I was in the middle of nowhere, deep in the jungle, at ten o' clock at night, surrounded by people I did not know, and about to be shot for something I knew nothing about. I could hear some of the women sobbing; the rest were silent. I stood with them, paralyzed: the priest, the religious, and the missionary, with a mantra playing in my head. "You will be shot like a dog and your body thrown into the jungle." The tape in my head kept playing and playing.

The officer strutted up and down in what might have been a comic pose, but for the terrifying reality of the setting.

"I will count to five to give you one last chance, and then I will shoot all of you if nobody comes forward. A very bad thing has happened, and you all will be punished. I will take pity on no one." He pronounced it as "piety," but I was under no illusion as to what he meant.

He spoke with the slow, precise over-articulation of a full-blown drunk. In those few minutes which could have been my last, I did not think of death, I did not think of God, I did not pray. I was listening to the tape "You will be shot like a dog and thrown into the jungle, you will be shot..." I could not believe that my life would end like this. It was all too unreal, that I was only seconds away from death.

"One, two, three...," taking his time and solemnly waving his arm up and down for each number, the officer began the countdown. Reflections from the headlights magnified his size, making him appear like some fairy tale ogre.

Suddenly, there was a distraction. Two soldiers burst out of the shack, obviously very drunk, each carrying a bottle of beer, one trying to pour it over the other. They were shouting and laughing. The officer glanced over at them and halted his count for a moment. And then I recognized it. These two were yelling in Hausa; they had all been speaking Hausa. I don't know what possessed me, but I stepped forward and shouted at them in their own language, "Brothers, I am from your country." It stopped them in their tracks.

They moved towards me. The officer peered at me. It was clear that up to that moment, none of them had recognized me as a white man. I jabbered as fast as I could, desperately reaching into my memory bank for every appropriate Hausa word and phrase I could remember, slowly moving further into the light so that they might see more clearly who I was. Even in the coolness of the night air, I could feel the sweat of terror all over my body, dripping from my chin, running down my neck.

"This is *Idoma* country and this mammy wagon is from *Igedde*, how can you speak our language? And what are you doing with these bad people?" they asked in amazement. (*Hausa was the first native language I had learned when I arrived in Nigeria.*)

"I am the Catholic priest from *Igedde*, and I need to get to Otrukpo. But I have lived in your country, in Keffi."

"I know where that place is," one of them said. Not to be outdone, the officer stated proudly, "I am a Christian, Reverend Father, and I know your people. All the Reverend Fathers are good people."

At this point, I had no idea where all this would lead, but I knew that for the moment the execution had been halted. I had become an object of curiosity. Clearly fascinated with this unusual phenomenon, they began gathering around me leaving the people standing against the wagon. The soldiers were all from the North, with the exception of the three whom I had first heard speaking and who turned out to be *Yoruba*. I didn't know one word of their language.

Native politeness soon took over, and I was asked, "Would the Reverend Father like a beer?" Without waiting for a response, one of them quickly produced a bottle, stuck it between his teeth, gave it a quick twist, spat out the metal cap, and handed the bottle to me. The warm beer bubbled out, running over my fingers feeling wet and sticky on my skin. I had trouble drinking from the bottle. I hadn't eaten all day and my stomach was in such a state that all I wanted to do was vomit. I couldn't stop my hands from shaking. I was also terrified that if they continued drinking, the situation would get out of control again.

In between small sips and using a mixture of Hausa and English, I tried to explain that this wagon was from my place and that I had been with it all day. I lied, "I know all of these people; they are from my parish."

"But these drivers and conductors go all over these areas cheating people," one of them insisted.

"You do not know how bad they are," commented the officer whom I could now see was simply a sergeant.

"Yes, but today I have been with them all the time. They have done no harm and it is night, so you need to let us go."

The sergeant paused for a moment, his bleary eyes falling half shut as if he was thinking deeply. He signaled for the group to move towards the hut, leaving me on my own with my back still towards the passengers. I desperately wanted to turn around to comfort them, to let them know that I was trying to get a solution. It was only then that I prayed, asking God to get us out of this terrible mess, and holding the bottle behind my back as discreetly as I could, I let the warm beer dribble down the back of my leg and out onto the ground.

After what seemed an awfully long time, but was probably just a couple of minutes, the sergeant approached me again, and in a slurry voice announced, "OK. You can go now, everybody except the conductor. He must stay for further questioning." *(Perhaps money was really at the bottom of it after all).* The soldiers came over and shook my hand. "Ah," said one of them, "you will need another beer for the journey." And with that, he

5

jammed another bottle between his teeth, opened it with a flick of the wrist, and with a big toothy grin thrust it into my hand. They all told me their names, as if somehow I would remember them kindly, and told me to 'Go with God' and finish my journey well.

We sat in complete silence as the soldier dragged the barrier open. I could sense that everyone on the wagon was in a state of shock and engrossed with their own thoughts. Once clear of the checkpoint, I quickly tossed the beer bottle into the bush.

As we entered Otrukpo, I asked the driver to drop my tires at the mechanic's shop in the marketplace, and to put me down at the crossroads. There was no electricity in the town, no street lights. There was no traffic. Most people were afraid to be out at night. I ran, stumbling through the darkness like a madman to the military police post that was near the mission. I quickly recounted my story to the officer on duty, saying that I feared for the conductor's life, but I had clearly wakened him from sleep. Responding laconically with an air of boredom, he said drowsily that he would have somebody check it out in the morning.

It took me less than five minutes running to reach the mission, but it was now close to midnight and the whole compound was in deep blackness, clearly locked up for the night. I hammered on the door for what seemed a long time, until finally a sleepy, grumpy, and nervous voice demanded, "Who is it and what do you want?"

"It's me, Frank, it's me, Mike Barrington and I need help." There was the sound of sliding bolts, as he struggled in the dark to get the door open.

"Holy Christ," he said, shining his flashlight on to my face, "it's my wee fucking priest. Mike, what's happened?" This mission still did not have its own generator, but I could clearly see Frank O'Donnell standing there, wearing just a pair of baggy shorts and a pair of sandals, his disheveled hair clearly indicating that I had gotten him out of bed.

"I was held up by the military at the checkpoint, and they gave me a rough time. I don't have my truck, so I've been traveling since early morning on a mammy wagon."

"Have you eaten?" he asked.

"No, I haven't eaten all day."

Without another word, he left me standing at the doorway in the dark, stormed over to a small house, and beat on the door hollering, "Joseph, come on out, you bastard. Leave your wife alone and get out here. My wee fucking priest is here and he needs something to eat."

The cook came out pulling on his shorts, briefly greeted me, and ran off to the kitchen to get a fire going.

Most of the rest of that night is a blur. Frank had built a shady place made of palm fronds in his yard where he could sit out, relax, and entertain. The local priests jokingly referred to it as the "throne room." It was cool and comfortable. After bringing me a cold beer, he insisted that I tell him everything in detail. I have no recollection of how many beers I drank that night or how long we sat outside, and I only vaguely remember falling into bed. I do recall, however, that in the beginning he kept asking me to "Take it slowly, Mike. Take it slowly, I want to hear everything."

I slept late and woke up at noon with a massive hangover. Frank insisted that I try and have some lunch with him, then sent me back to bed for a siesta. That evening after he'd taken me downtown to retrieve my tires, he insisted that I stay with him for a couple of days.

"I'd love to, Frank," I replied, "but I'm sure that Wally, my new boss, will be worried about me, especially if I don't show up at all."

"God almighty," he said with a laugh, "you think that that old fart can't manage on his own for a while without you? I'll send a driver to him with a message to let him know things are fine."

The following day as we were enjoying a drink in the "throne room" before lunch, he was in his classic pose, bush hat pushed back on his head, his right hand grasping a whiskey 'on the rocks', and his long legs fully stretched out with his feet resting on the low table in front of him. Looking me straight in the eye, he spoke softly in his Scottish highland lilt, "Mike, laddie, do you want to go back to Igedde?" Before I could respond, he held up his hand as if to silence me. "You don't have to answer me just now and you need to hear it from me: you don't have to go back to the bush if you don't want to. It's perfectly OK."

It had never entered my mind not to go back, so I told him, "I'm ready, Frank. If you can get me a ride, I'll go back in the morning."

In typical fashion, eyes twinkling, he took a sip of his whiskey, then said with a smile, "I thought you would, you little asshole. You're so fucking romantic."

And so I did.

Of all the men I met in Nigeria or anywhere else, Frank O'Donnell stands alone. He was one truly great priest and a "braw Scot" in every sense of the word. He had lived and trekked the bush for years, knew the hardships of missionary life and had proven himself to be a real leader of men. His legacy of churches, schools, and clinics that he had built all over the diocese was there for all to see. He hated war, was nervous around the gun-toting, sometimes unpredictable soldiers, and was not afraid to say so. (Otrukpo was the end of the railway line, and thousands of armed troops engulfed the town daily waiting for transport to the front.) His hospitality was legendary, as was his use of the Queen's English. His honesty and integrity were admired by all who came into contact with him. His parishioners worshipped him.

But he was out of favor with the politics of the new Bishop and his focus on younger men with newer ideas. While preparing to go home on a much needed furlough, he learned that a younger man would be replacing him in Otrukpo. Already "demoted" from the cathedral parish of Makurdi, the most important post in the diocese, Frank made a radical, and what must have been a very difficult decision. He left Nigeria and never returned. He died less than three years later.

Frank was the very first priest I had met that day I arrived in Makurdi and he left an indelible impression on me. By local standards, the town where he ministered was large with a population of nearly 10,000. The narrow, black-top road shimmering in the midday heat cut a contrasting swath through the green jungle as it snaked its way over a steeply winding hill. And suddenly there it was spread out below us: a rambling collection of rusty, corrugated iron roofs poking through steaming, dense, verdant vegetation and swaying palm trees, all huddled together against the backdrop of the wide, brown, slow-flowing Benue River. As we descended still lower onto the flood plain itself, the searing heat and energy-sapping humidity left me drenched with sweat. I had learned so much about this place during all of my years in training, seen countless slide shows and photos and heard about it from dozens of returning missionaries that, in a strange sort of way, I felt I was coming home.

Makurdi was the administrative capital of the region and also the Catholic headquarters, home of the new Bishop-elect, Seamus Foley. He was dressed in a long, Episcopal, white cassock edged with a narrow band of purple, but he still had the same bald head and "piggy" eyes I remembered from my high school days when he was one of my professors.

"Welcome to Makurdi, Father Barrington," he said in a very formal manner, "I hope you did not have too much trouble with the military. We have been waiting for you." He was seated in his office on the second floor of a modestly sized, but attractive house situated in a lovely park-like setting. I couldn't help but notice the beautiful, and to me unusually colorful, flowering, tropical shrubs that were everywhere. Rising to greet me, his podgy offered hand felt like the proverbial wet fish.

He was brief, businesslike, and to the point. Keeping us standing the whole time, he said, "I'm sure you will not be too happy with this information, but I am assigning you to teach at the junior seminary in Keffi. They are desperately short of qualified personnel."

Fortunately, this did not come as a total surprise to me, for my driving companion Ron had already given me a heads up on the posting. But I still wanted it to be known that after thirteen years of college, I did not want to spend my days in a classroom.

As if to anticipate my response he continued, holding up the palm of his outstretched hand towards me, "I know you are eager to work in a parish, and I will reassign you just as soon as I can, but meanwhile I hope that you will understand. I believe that your transportation to Keffi will be provided for you at the mission, and I'm sure you will get a meal there." I was struggling with the heat and would have really liked any kind of cold drink, even water, but none was offered, and I did not feel comfortable enough to ask for one.

"Unfortunately, we have just finished our lunch, and my cook has already left," the Bishop continued. "However, I would like you to join us for a drink this evening."

"Thank you, Bishop," I said softly.

Then turning to my companion, he smiled and said, "You know the routine, Ron; I assume you will bring him along."

"Sure thing, Seamus," Ron responded and then immediately checked himself. "I'm so sorry, Bishop, I didn't mean…"

"Don't worry about it, Ron," he said with a chuckle. "We're both going to have to get used to my new title. I'll see you later."

9

This whole encounter felt strange to me as I struggled with negative memories from my adolescent days. My past had suddenly caught me unawares, and I was striving to handle my own deep feelings about this man. My prior experience of him had not been pleasant. Officious, and full of his own importance, as a high school professor he had given us the impression that he was there for his own self-importance, and not for the benefit of his students. I tried to put these memories behind me, telling myself that it was just ancient history. I was the only priest in the diocese who had experienced him in that capacity and it soon became clear that I needed to keep my thoughts, feelings, and experiences on this subject to myself.

"Is he always that stuffy?" I asked Ron as we drove away.

"Well, no," he replied hesitantly. "I think Seamus is trying to find his level. Don't forget, he hasn't yet been formally inducted as Bishop of Makurdi. And also, you need to know that we were without a Bishop for a long time. The priests out here couldn't agree on a candidate, and Rome actually had to step in to make the final decision."

For a second, Ron was distracted: he was forced to swerve the truck suddenly to avoid a large herd of Fulani cattle that had just appeared out of the bush and was starting to cross the road directly in front of us. Their owners, hands hooked on long sticks across their shoulders, raised a few fingers in greeting and continued ambling nonchalantly along as if the whole road belonged to them.

"So Seamus must be somewhat unsure of himself," Ron continued, apparently unfazed by the near accident. "He knows that he has a great deal of work to do towards reunification. Also, prior to his election, he was principal of the largest teacher training college in Nigeria and was very much one of the boys. He loved to party. Perhaps he's now realizing that he has to learn how to be a Bishop, and I guess this formality is one way of distancing himself from his past. I really don't know. Only time will tell."

This was a piece of important history, and I was glad he shared it with me. It was troubling and also clear that I needed a crash course in the politics of this diocese, and the sooner the better in order to avoid some serious faux pas. It was strange hearing all of this and difficult to fully absorb as I was so mesmerized by my surroundings. Sweat-covered people were everywhere, jostling each other and pushing their home-made hand carts, some weighed down with bananas and five gallon silver-colored cans (which Ron informed me were filled with kerosene), and others with stacks of galvanized sheeting. Women wrapped in gaily colored cloth were walking by, their neck muscles taut with the weight of the heavy loads on their heads, the sweat on their faces and shoulders glistening in the bright sunlight. I asked Ron to stop for a photo: one woman was carrying a huge basin on her head filled with rice and with a little child sitting on top, a "Kodak moment" for sure. The woman giggled as Ron spoke to her in Tiv, asking her permission.

The Makurdi central mission suddenly came into view on a rise a half mile down the road from the Bishop's compound, alongside a large church that served as the cathedral for the diocese. I was surprised to see that the church was built with European-style bricks, and Ron informed me that German missionaries had built it in the thirties, and had taught the locals not only how to manufacture bricks, but also how to build with them. Next to the church was the residence of the Vicar General, Frank O'Donnell.

He stood waiting for us on the verandah of an imposing modern, two story mission house that he himself had built. Frank was in his typical John Wayne pose: hands on hips, sporting a rather crumpled, sweat-stained, short sleeved, white shirt, long khaki bush shorts and knee-length white socks. A Stetson was stuck on the back of his head and the smoking remains of a cheroot clamped between his teeth. A grin the size of the Grand Canyon spread across his craggy, sunburned face.

"How's my wee fucking priest?" was his greeting, as this tall well built man with the most piercing blue eyes I had ever seen, came down the steps, crushed my hand with a vice-like grip, and gave me a slap on the back that almost left me breathless. "You're welcome, Michael. You're welcome, laddie," he announced in his lilting Scots accent.

"Christ, Ron, you old bastard," he said, turning to my companion and treating him to a similar greeting, "What kept you? I've been expecting you all morning. I thought perhaps you had been held up at one of the sodding checkpoints outside of town. They've been giving us a lot of grief these past few days. Bishop Delisle from Ankpa was here the other day, and had his tires shot from under him by some bastard of a drunken soldier."

"Hi, Frank," said Ron, giving him a big bear hug. "No, we had a pretty good trip, but we spent some time at the Bishop's house."

"Ah, so that asshole Foley is more important than me," he joked; "now all you want is my food and my fucking beer. Come inside, both of you, and make yourselves at home. I have some urgent military shit I need to attend to and will be back shortly." With that he strode purposefully towards a dusty, dark blue Peugeot pickup truck, almost identical to our own, parked in the shade a huge mango tree and drove off to the sound of crunching gears and spinning tires.

During his twenty-five years in Nigeria, Frank had established himself as a real supporter and leader of men. His hospitality was known to all, and in this very stressful time of civil war, in a diocese without a Bishop for several years, he had shouldered all of the responsibility for sixty priests and nuns in this huge territory of almost 15,000 square miles

An airy dining room on the ground floor, its windows and doors open wide in an effort to catch any whisper of breeze that might occur, held a noisy group of about twelve people enjoying lunch. As we entered, Joe O'Neil, a heavy set, balding, middle-aged man, the only priest among them, and a twenty-five year veteran, jumped to his feet.

"Welcome, Michael. Welcome. Come in, grab a chair and have some lunch. I'm now as deaf as a post, but if you speak directly to me I can lip read. I'm your driver and will take you to the Keffi. We'll leave in a couple of hours. We're just about finished, but there's plenty for you and Ron, and for Frank when he returns."

He quickly introduced us to the other people present: members of Catholic Relief Services, Oxfam, and the International Red Cross. While they smiled and welcomed us, they all looked tired and worn out. The only topic of conversation was the progress of the war and the problems and difficulties of dealing with the military, which constantly hindered their efforts to deliver humanitarian aid, mainly food and medical supplies. For these organizations, the Catholic missions up and down the only service-able road in the area were centers of support, distribution, and frequently a meal, a shower, and a bed.

Frank, looking tense and tired, returned just as Ron and I were finishing our meal. By this time everybody else had left.

"Why don't you two stick around and give me the latest news while I eat?" he said, tossing his bush hat on the table. The heavy dining chair suddenly slipped from his grasp as he dragged it from under the table, and fell on its side. As he bent down to retrieve it, I couldn't help but notice his face, which now that I was closer, looked sunken and hollow under his dark tan. There were deep lines etched into his cheeks and large dark blotches under his eyes. This man was exhausted.

"But Joe is taking me to the junior seminary," I informed him, "He told me we would be leaving soon."

"Don't worry about that old bastard, Michael," he said, finally flopping onto his chair. "He never in his life went anywhere without first taking a fucking siesta. Trust me, he won't be moving for at least a couple of hours. And in any case, I want you to relax and spend the night here with me, so what the hell. Ron, will you please tell the old bugger when he wakes up that he can travel to Keffi in the morning?"

"That's great," replied Ron, "because Seamus has invited us over to his place this evening for a cocktail hour."

As if he had not heard Ron, Frank continued.

"These military fuckers are so difficult to work with at times, but thank God there are still some good ones around," he mumbled as Ali, his cook, shuffled in with his food and a cold beer. When Ali leaned over, I was riveted by the deep tribal markings on his heavily lined face: long symmetrical cicatrices almost from the ear to the corner of his mouth that looked as if the flesh had been gouged out. He caught me looking at him and smiled knowingly but warmly, revealing what I could see as rows of filed teeth.

"I was lucky to find a major who understood my situation," Frank said. "But, oh! You guys probably have no clue what I am talking about." He felt the bottle to check if it was really cold, then slowly and deliberately poured the contents into his glass. His face revealed that his thoughts were elsewhere. Then quickly taking a gulp, and clearly but briefly savoring its contents, he continued.

"Three days ago, that stupid asshole McKay managed to overturn his truck. Can you believe it? That's what happens when you put a college jackass into a bush parish. He only learned to drive a month ago. Anyway, he is in the hospital with a suspected broken neck, and I need to get him out of here and back to the UK as soon as possible. What a fucking mess! It would be difficult enough even without this sodding war."

"This is terrible news," Ron said, leaning forward and listening more intently. "Is there anything that I can do to help, Frank? There is no way

McKay can be transported to Kano airport (*the nearest international airport four hundred and fifty miles away*). I would be willing to take him, but the roads are so bad the trip would probably kill him."

"Thanks, but no Ron. I've taken care of it. Luckily there's an air force major I know stationed at the field. That's where I've just been. He graduated from one of my schools years ago, and fortunately he remembered me kindly and I'm happy that I hadn't totally pissed him off. Tomorrow he'll have McKay flown up to Kano, and I'll go with him. He even let me use a military phone to make arrangements with British Airways who are prepared to handle a stretcher case. He'll be back in the UK within forty-eight hours."

"Wow!" Ron exclaimed, "you're a miracle worker, Frank. Thank God you're here! But how will you let our people in England know that they have a seriously injured priest about to arrive on their doorstep?"

"Shit! What else can I do from down here?" Frank exploded in exasperation, throwing both his knife and fork down with a clatter. "It's such a fucking God-awful country! Nothing works when you need it. Christ almighty! There are no bloody phones, no telegraph, pieces of shit for roads, and now a fucking new Bishop who has never lived in the bush, never had to deal with a crisis, and doesn't know his ass from his elbow. It will have to wait until I get to Kano, and then hopefully, I'll be able to get through to London." This sudden and unexpected outburst left both Ron and me dumbstruck.

"And as if this was my only worry!" He brooded, pausing for just a few moments, but they seemed like an eternity to me. He stared into his beer glass, his right hand bunched into a tight fist, clenching his knife, looking as if he was about to smash it through the four-inch solid mahogany table.

"Why is it that some men simply can't keep their dicks in their pants?" he murmured to himself slowly shaking his head. "Screwing around with women out here is one thing; it's not good and I have known lots of it, but messing around with school kids…." There was a longer pause. "I simply don't get it. Not only do I not get it, I feel like killing the bastard."

Neither Ron nor I said a word; there was no need. In any event, I wouldn't have known what to say. I was somewhat in shock and struggling to follow all of it. This kind of openness and honesty was so strange and new to me, I felt like an intruder. My interest was piqued but at the same time I felt terribly uncomfortable. Is this the sort of stuff I would be regularly exposed to out here, I wondered? Nothing in my seminary training had prepared me for this. It had simply never come up as a topic of either conversation or class discussion.

"Earlier this morning I fired Ted Goodman the principal of St. Anthony's High School for Boys," he said, dropping his voice again. "He is already on his way to the airport, the bastard. I hope he never makes it," he snorted, his eyes beginning to flash again, his voice intense as he spat out the words. "I hope he gets shot by some fucking drunken soldier."

"Goodman has been screwing around sexually, literally fucking around with some of his students for months, and we did not know about it. I only heard about it a couple of days ago." He leaned back in his chair as if reliving the scene again. He held his interlocked fingers for a moment behind his head, revealing his huge muscular biceps, starkly white in contrast to his bronzed forearms, then stretched his fingers upwards, brought them over his head and forward, and then cracked them, the sound amplified by our silence. Reaching for his glass, he took another long, slow, mouthful of beer and continued.

"Some students complained to the Vice Principal that certain boys were getting very high grades and yet were not studying like the rest of the kids. Each of these boys was confronted, and one of them gave us all the details. You can figure out the rest of the story. In all of my years out here I have never, never had a priest of mine fuck around like this. The bastard should be castrated. And frankly, I don't give a shit what the boss back in the UK does with him; I just want him out of my territory. I can only hope that he will be put in a place where he can no longer do any harm."

Frank must have sensed our increasing unease, for he brusquely pushed his plate towards the center of the table, muttering, "Oh hell! I can't eat this shit."

There was a long pause as he held the remainder of his beer, looking into the glass for some time, slowly swirling the foamy golden liquid around and around. Then with a quick gulp it was suddenly gone, and in a second his old business-like self returned.

"I need to get over to the hospital to let McKay and the nurses know that he will be leaving with the military in the morning," he said, making a grab for his hat. "I don't want them shitting themselves when the military medics arrive, complete with armed escort, to cart him off. They might think some nasty negative thing is about to happen." He burst out laughing at his own dark sense of humor.

"Do you want to join me, Ron?" he enquired with just sufficient intimation in his voice that it was clearly a request.

Without any hesitation, Ron responded, "Of course I do."

Frank's chair scraped on the cement floor as he quickly came to his feet. Then pausing momentarily, he looked directly at me with an intensity that took me completely by surprise.

"Michael, laddie, I want you to know that this mission will always be a home for you," he emphasized, thumping the table with his clenched fist. "And don't pay any attention to people who might say otherwise. They are just full of shit, and there is lots of that in this diocese. The diocese needs you. Good luck in the seminary and my best wishes to your family when you write home." And with that he stuck his well-worn bush hat on the back of his head, stopped for a few seconds to light up a cheroot, strode out onto the verandah, and was gone.

The reception at the Bishop's house that evening was a completely new experience for me. There were about twelve people present, among them a loud young army colonel, a former student of the Bishop who was the life and soul of the party, and two junior officers. Four Swiss Red Cross workers who spoke primarily French were delighted I could converse with them, and there were three Canadian nuns, nurses dressed in slacks, all of whom smoked incessantly and drank gin and tonic. A young air force major with his beautiful wife, and a young, "hippy type" American photographer rounded out the group. The latter, in the middle of the reception, decided that the best thing for his aching back was to lie down in the middle of the floor. Nobody passed any comment on this, to my mind, rather odd behavior or seemed to care in the least about it. But my most vivid memory of that evening was of the Bishop himself casually walking over to a corner of the verandah, still talking to a small group over his shoulder, hoisting up his white cassock around his hips revealing his short, white, ankle-socks, pink legs, and khaki shorts, and then casually peeing into the night. I had learned that this was standard procedure in order to save water, but what made this rather different, was that it was accompanied by loud sound effects. The reception was taking place on an outside patio on the second floor.

CHAPTER 2

Community Living

"Welcome," Michael. "You're very welcome." Barney O'Reilly, a bald-headed, pale-faced, bespectacled, gentle-looking man, the rector of the seminary and my new boss approached me, stepping down from the verandah and holding out his hand. "Everybody calls me Barney." he announced laughingly. "I think you might have met most of the others," he said, waving a very white hand in the direction of the four casually dressed men approaching the truck. "But come on in, you must be tired," and looking at my once white cassock, now heavily stained with red dust, quickly added, "You'll probably feel better after a shower."

At that moment the sounds of a generator filled the air, and suddenly the campus and all its buildings were flooded with light. A myriad of flying insects magically appeared as if from nowhere and started buzzing around our heads, but then headed for the bright wall light above the double doors on the patio.

"Eh our kid, how's Manchester United doing? You're welcome Michael." Dennis Cartwright a friend of my family, who had been in the seminary with my uncle, held out a tanned spindly hand to me. He had no family of his own and visited my parents each time he was on leave, so

I had met him several times. I was shocked at how emaciated he looked with dark sunken eyes and hollow cheeks. He was dressed in a very dirty, once-white tank top with a large ink stain on the front, over which hung a case holding his glasses. It was clear that he hadn't shaved for several days. A faded black French beret covered his balding head but not all of his hair, which stuck out unevenly in graying, greasy tufts. His wardrobe was completed by a pair of dirty, blue shorts and sandals made from old tires. This skinny, gaunt and unkempt "brother" looked like he needed a good scrubbing, and for some reason I couldn't get the image of Mark Twain's Tom Sawyer out of my mind. I didn't know it at the time, but Dennis was in the throes of a nervous breakdown.

"Hey, Den. It's good to see you" I responded, his claw-hand in mine feeling literally like skin and bone.

"Well then, grab your bag that's got a clean shirt in it, and I'll show you your room. The boys will get the rest of your baggage."

I was especially happy to re-connect with Paddy Gaffney, a Scot from Glasgow. We had been together in the seminary and although he was a couple of years ahead of me, he proved to be a true friend. He had put on a little weight since I last saw him, but he still had the same freckled smiling face and flaming red hair with a temper to match. I was to learn that he had spent the previous year in Igedde, which later on would be my first real bush parish assignment. He was as dissatisfied as I was, probably even more so, at being assigned to a teaching position. We would, however, work well together in the coming months.

"Mike, it's so good to see you." I was crushed in a bear hug that felt genuine and warm. "You have the room next to mine. We'll be able to talk later. I want to hear all the news from the UK."

"Hell, Paddy, I wasn't expecting to see you here. What did you do wrong to deserve this posting?" I kidded. "I'm so happy you're here. This is such a great surprise."

Another priest slowly emerged out of the shadows. Quite unlike the others, he was immaculately dressed in a clean, white, short sleeved sports shirt, with ridiculous-looking starched and creased, long khaki shorts that came well below his knees, along with white stockinged feet ensconced in what looked like a very comfortable pair of black leather sandals. This apparition was JP Brady, a tall, graying, aloof-looking and bespectacled man in his fifties. Holding his prayer book in one hand, and looking as if he resented being disturbed, he extended a flaccid hand.

"My, oh my," he mused, his squinting eyes scrutinizing me from head to toe, making me feel as if I was back in boarding school in the headmaster's study, "You don't resemble your uncle at all!"

Jackie Taylor, the last member of the group, perhaps sensing the awkwardness of the moment quickly chimed in, "You're very welcome Michael."

"Hi to both of you," I said, shaking their hands.

"Here, Michael, let me help you with your bag."

Without waiting, Jackie, a tall, blond haired but slightly stooped giant of a man reached over and grabbed my backpack. His arms were exceedingly long and I noticed his hands: they were huge like those of a professional boxer.

"Follow me," he said, softly. And with that he padded off in the direction of the open French windows and my room.

"Here you are, Michael. You'll find everything you need for the shower, and it's just outside your door. You'll share it with Paddy."

It was only as he left me alone, that I realized his gentle voice covered a slight speech impediment; he had a stutter.

It had all happened whirlwind fast, but I had just met all the members of my new, religious community.

I had only been in Keffi a week or so, when there was a discussion in my English class about learning and languages. I was surprised that so many tribes were represented, and that most of these fourteen-year-old kids were multi-lingual. Amazingly, none of them had ever studied any language in a book. I asked them if it was easy to learn a native language and indicated that I was very eager to start. I was especially keen to learn Hausa, the main local language and the lingua franca for the whole of Northern Nigeria. I told them that Dennis was my teacher, and that I had given myself six months to be able to speak, read, and write it fluently!

All of sudden a voice from the back of the class piped up. "Slow, slow catch monkey, Father."

"What do you mean?" I asked.

The young Tiv student stood up. "In my tribe when men go hunting, if they really want to catch a monkey, they have to approach it very slowly

19

and carefully. It can sometimes take a long time just to find it, and monkeys are very difficult to catch. They are very cunning, and simply cannot be rushed. My brother is a good hunter and he taught me. It can take time to get what you really want."

I would never forget these words, and they would eventually become a touchstone for the rest of my life.

Dennis had a great sense of humor, joked around in public and was considered the "clown prince" of the diocese. Nobody took him seriously, so he had never held any position of real authority or responsibility, which was why he lived at the seminary. He was pastor of the local parish, but managed it from his room. Although we never talked about deep subjects (he was very much "old school" where dealing with or revealing one's feelings and intimate issues was a sign of weakness), he was fun to be with. Still, I think basically he was a very lonely man, and his clowning filled a big hole inside of him. As I learned over the next few years, he was also unique. He had a great, natural facility for native languages, and in a diocese where priests typically did not speak them, Dennis was completely fluent in three: Hausa, Idoma, and Tiv.

"Hey, our kid," he said to me one morning as were going over a Hausa grammar book, "you asked me where you could get a pair of leather snake boots last night. I know the very person to go to. Why don't we take a walk together downtown? I have an al hadji friend who will take care of you."

"Sounds great to me," I replied, reaching for my sun glasses and bush hat. "Let's do it."

Going out with Dennis was always interesting. He laughed and joked with almost every person he met, and as they responded, I wasn't sure if it was his sense of humor, or simply the way he looked that they were laughing at.

It was also my first real visit to an old Nigerian town. Keffi was a small decrepit place that went back to about 1790, established by Abdul Zanga, a Fulani warrior from the north. It had originally made its name as a slave trading center. In the past, it had boasted the most beautiful mosque in the area and an emir's palace, but both now looked shabby and needing repair. A very narrow, pot-holed main street led directly to the town center, where it ended in front of the "palace" and a large twelve-foot high stone obelisk. Keffi had been a sort of "Wild West" frontier town, and in 1902 when the

British took over the control of the area, the locals rebelled and beheaded the administrator, a certain Captain Maloney. In addition to hanging the culprits, the British forced the emir to build this impressive, if somewhat incongruous monument in his memory. There was a small hospital and a GRA (*Government Reservation Area*) up on a small hill where some federal officials lived, and there was also a GC (Government College). I was on a fast track to learning the vocabulary of every Nigerian missionary which consisted of an amazing kind of shorthand, and a dictionary of acronyms: PWD, PO, STP, NPF, FPF, SDE, SUM, SIM, etc. The list was seemingly endless.

In the late morning heat, the dusty, ramshackle, open-front stores on each side of the road appeared quiet and devoid of customers. Occasionally, a blast of loud music pierced the air and broke the morning's tranquility. A couple of skinny, hobbled donkeys foraged through the garbage alongside the open drains, their mangy ears constantly twitching, irritated by swarms of scavenging flies. There was no sense of future business hustle and bustle here, more of a pace of life gently receding into the past.

Dennis suddenly darted off to the right into a narrow dark alley where the buildings almost touched each other. It resembled a maze as this passage fed into a whole series of others, like a giant sand-colored octopus. Only occasional patches of sunlight penetrated the dimness, and the air felt much cooler and comfortable.

He halted outside a small doorway with unusually carved wooden posts. A roughly hewn door stained with red, intricate, Hausa designs led into a cool, almost square room with a high ceiling. Even before I entered, I was impressed with the thickness of the mud walls, probably about two feet thick, and I heard chanting. They were clearly boys' voices, singing in unison, and they were young.

A bearded old man, wearing the traditional, flowing robe, an embroidered but dirty-white riga, and a full turban that draped around a red fez and under his chin, was sitting on a low, small, painted chair tooling a piece of leather. His kindly eyes sparkled with recognition, as he silently signaled to a small boy to bring stools from the next room.

"God be with you, al hadji Bandura," said Dennis in Hausa, bending low and touching a hand to his chest. A couple of minutes were spent as each of them went through an intricate exchange of greetings like some form of litany.

21

Dennis must have indicated who I was, for the old man suddenly gave me a big, toothless smile and announced in perfect English, "A blessing on you my friend, you are welcome to my home."

"A blessing on you too, al hadji," I responded.

"My friend here says you wish to have some boots. I will surely make them for you. Please," he said, taking a piece of cardboard carton from behind his chair and laying it on the ground in front of him, "remove your shoe and place your foot here." Taking a pencil he drew the outline of my foot. I was about to remove my other shoe when he gently chided me, "It is not necessary, I will simply turn this piece over." Then taking a pair of what looked like homemade shears, he cut out the pattern.

"And how tall do you want the boot?" he asked, carefully cutting off a long one-inch strip of cardboard.

I indicated a place about an inch and a half below my knee. The old man placed the strip against the side of my leg and snipped it at the appropriate height.

"That is all, thank you; I have some very fine goat leather. Your boots will be ready in two days, God willing."

I was amazed at the simplicity of it all.

Over the next hour we exchanged stories, and I learned that he had spent five years in the British army, and that he was also a master leather worker. He was surrounded by eight small boys. All were sitting cross-legged on the soft floor, and in front of each one was a board about twelve inches high and eight inches wide, supported by a small handle stuck into the sand. They were totally silent, no one speaking a word, not even looking at each other. Each was totally occupied sewing or stitching together small pieces of leather.

"And who are these boys?" I asked. "What are they doing?"

He briefly spoke to the group and immediately they began to chant in unison. *So this was the choir, I said to myself.* The old man sat, head bowed as if listening intently.

After about a minute, he suddenly held up his hand, and the singing stopped.

"These are my students," he stated proudly. "They will be with me for six years and during that time I will teach them everything about leather. They will be able to cure it, dye it, tool it, and make boots, shoes, saddles and bridles for our horses, scabbards for swords and daggers, anything that can be made out of leather." His face glowed with the pride and passion of a true craftsman. "And when I am finished, every student will know the whole of the Koran by heart. This is what I am teaching them; this is what they are singing."

"But what is the point of learning it by heart?" I replied." They are just small boys and cannot possibly understand it."

With a look of gentle compassion, as if for someone less fortunate than himself, Bandura responded, "Ah, you are correct, but they will all have the rest of their lives to pray and live it."

Once he knew that I was eager to understand the Koran and learn Hausa, he offered to be my teacher, and we became fast friends. I tried as often as possible to visit him twice a week; I was fascinated by his stories of Hausa history while improving my language skills. But I also learned much more from this kind old man. Before I left Keffi, I took him a gift of a hen and some eggs, a token gesture of thanks for all of his kindness. He graciously took them from me, called out to one of his wives, and told her to prepare food and give it to the poor.

"You are my honored son," he said chiding me gently. "Everything in this house is yours. You must not thank me for it."

Dennis's behavior was becoming more and more bizarre by the day. He was convinced that the "wash man" who did our laundry was bent on stealing his vest and shorts, and so he didn't want to change his clothes. Barney had to intervene, and then Dennis resorted to trying to wash his own clothes. The whole issue of the civil war was getting to him. There were heavily armed military personnel everywhere and checkpoints all around the town. While this created an air of tension for all of us, we were never directly bothered by them. JP Brady was openly pro-Ibo (the predominately Catholic tribe in the breakaway State of Biafra) and several times during the day, and especially in the evening when we would gather for a drink before dinner, he would walk up and down outside with a small portable radio listening to banned Ibo pirate radio stations. His reason was that he needed to get, as he said, the "true news." He was so openly hostile and critical of the Nigerian Federal Government that he made all of us very nervous.

Dennis in particular found him difficult to deal with, especially the flaunting of his pro-Ibo sympathies. He was afraid somebody might report

JP to the authorities, perhaps a cook, a houseboy, or a student, and then we would all be deported. Dennis' paranoia started to become more evident by the day. At night, he checked and double checked all the doors and windows for security. When he spoke, it was in hushed tones so that nobody else within earshot could hear anything. Other than saying Mass on Sunday for the parish and showing up for dinner in the evening, he hid himself in his room. He was now sporting a grey and black scraggly beard, so Paddy nicknamed him "Gabby" Hayes, after the famous Western film actor. Against the Rector's wishes, but out of necessity, Paddy and I agreed to take over the parish for him until a replacement could be found.

Dennis needed to go home, but there was a major problem: he was afraid to fly. He wanted to take a ship from Lagos which he had done several times before. He also preferred a berth on a merchant ship which would mean a journey of several weeks. The problem for Barney, the Rector, was how to get him to Lagos, a daunting and difficult proposition. We were in the midst of a civil war: the nearest railway station was four hours away across the bush on a dirt road, and the station at Minna itself was about five hundred miles from Lagos. I was delegated to drive Dennis to the station, and to make sure that he got on the train!

"Are you sure you want me to take him?" I asked Barney when we were alone in the sitting room, having a coffee between classes one day.

"Yes, Mike. Dennis has taken a real liking to you, and somehow trusts you."

I was a bag of nerves thinking about the trip, and the numerous military check-points I would encounter. It was especially difficult not knowing how Dennis would handle the tension of it all.

My problems really started once we reached the city limits of Minna. It was noontime and I wanted to head to the central mission for lunch, knowing that the train was not due until later that evening. Dennis had removed his beret and was now repeatedly twisting and untwisting it as if it were wet and he wanted to wring it out.

"Hey, our kid," he began, with a quiver in his voice that showed me he was beginning to stress out, "I think we should go and check if the train is on time."

"But Den," I responded, "it won't be here for another six hours. We have lots of time to take care of things."

"Yes, our kid, but you don't know this country yet. Perhaps the station master will refuse to sell me a ticket."

"OK," I agreed. Just to pacify him and since the station was quite near the mission, I made the detour.

Dennis jumped out of the truck and ran into the station-master's office, almost before I had time to park properly. Following him into the deserted ticket office, I heard him being assured that, "Yes, the train is on schedule. There is only one train today"

"Then I need to purchase a ticket to Lagos." Dennis was still wearing the very same clothes I had seen him in the day I arrived in Keffi, with one exception; now he had added a faded, khaki, multi-pocketed bush jacket with the sleeves crudely cut off at the shoulder. Fumbling inside his dirty vest, he extracted a small, cloth purse held around his neck with a black shoelace. Although we were the only people at the ticket counter, Dennis shuffled off to the furthest corner of the room, and with his back turned to us, extracted his money. It took all of fifteen minutes for the clerk, in true Nigerian fashion, to produce the correct ticket, and I felt certain, that if the station master had not been present, the offer of an appropriate "dash" would have been clearly requested.

The town of Minna was sizzling under a cloudless sky and a gentle breeze that only seemed to fan the heat. It was the height of the dry season, and the temperature must have been well over one hundred degrees. I decided that we would head off to the local mission for a cold beer and some lunch. Since we now knew the exact time of the train's arrival, (it wasn't due in until six o'clock) and it was a real dog-day afternoon, I thought that we should take a siesta, but it was not to be. Dennis became more and more agitated. Now he was terrified that he would miss the train. He obsessed about it through the whole meal, insisting that after lunch I drive him back to the station to check again on its arrival. Even the elderly, very kind and experienced Monsignor with whom we had lunch could not convince him that we had plenty of time.

Soon Dennis switched his obsessing. "Kid, you do not know this country," he kept repeating, "and trains can stop at any time and for any reason. It might not get here today."

In spite of my protestations and assurances that the train was on schedule, he insisted that I take him back to the station, just to check on things once more. The station was only about five minutes away from the mission, and I ended up driving him there almost every hour. At one point, after asking the station master yet again if the train was on time, and again being reassured that it was, Dennis looked as if he was about to cry.

"Hey, our kid, I don't think he is telling us the truth. Do you? I don't think there is a train today, and he has taken my money for himself."

"No, Den," I explained, "you are holding an official ticket and it is stamped for today. I even heard the telegraph operator (I lied) talking with the Kagoro station master. He said that the train had already left. It will be here on time, Den."

I did eventually put him on the train, but deep inside I wondered how he would manage in Lagos if he failed to connect with the person meeting him. There was a forlorn quality to this "goodbye." There he was, this skinny, shrunken, nervous, beaten man, waving and smiling at me, beret on his head, an unlit pipe clamped between his stained teeth, his scraggly beard wafting in the breeze through the open carriage window, still wearing that same dirty tank top with the huge ink stain on the front and the same homemade sandals on his feet. *And I wondered, "Is this what Africa does to a man after twenty years in the bush? Is this what I am in for?"*

JP Brady was becoming more and more critical of our approach to mission work, and Paddy found it difficult to tolerate him. To me he was just a nagging bitter "old woman" who was angry about the many changes taking place in the Church. He found it "shocking" that Paddy and I read our breviary, the priests' daily prayer book, in English instead of Latin. As the bursar of the seminary, he was also in charge of all finances and material purchases including food. While our meals were generally quite good, he exercised strict control over the amount and kind of food we could take on safari.

"This food costs money, you know. There's a war going on," were among his favorite expressions.

He quickly showed himself to be a mean, vindictive, and embittered priest who made no attempt to coach us or share his twenty years of missionary experience with us, preferring to criticize our efforts and dampen our youthful enthusiasm. In his eyes, the civil war was simply a religious jihad; the Muslim biased Federal Government trying to defeat the largely Catholic breakaway Biafran Government. He constantly criticized us and the rest of the priests in the diocese for our lack of support for Biafra. I was soon to learn firsthand, however, that this priest, who said Mass every day, prayed in public, and visited the sick in the local hospital was not everything he purported to be.

My first experience of malaria, about which I had heard, read, and learned so much since we all took a prophylactic against it daily, came when Paddy and I had been out in the bush for a day or so, visiting a small school and church. I was excited to be learning from him how to go on safari, live in the bush, and do what every missionary had come to Africa to do: to evangelize, share the Good News, and help those less fortunate than ourselves in any way possible.

At about noon on the second day during which we had to leave our truck and hike for several hours under a blistering sun, to a fairly remote village called Kukuri, I knew something was seriously wrong. I was sitting under a tree hearing the confessions of some school kids when he came to me and said,

"Mike, you've got to get me out of here. I'm feeling terrible." This was not like Paddy at all. He was young, strong, and healthy, and definitely not the type to complain.

"What's the problem?" I asked.

"I just feel terrible and have a blinding headache," he replied. "I've also got the 'shivers'."

I knew it was serious because the temperature must have been in the nineties and he was even wearing his white cassock. I immediately told the catechist and head teacher that I was leaving with Paddy because he was sick, and would return as soon as possible.

The hike back to the truck must have seemed like an eternity to Paddy. We stopped several times because he needed to throw up. At first we said nothing, but concentrated on walking as fast as we could. He was perspiring heavily, yet complained constantly of shivering. It was about thirty miles to the seminary, and as soon as I hit the heavily, pot-holed dirt road, I drove as fast as I could. This was the dry season, and we traveled in a cloud of choking red dust. The rattling of the truck as it bumped along made conversation almost impossible.

Paddy sat with his eyes closed, continuing to sweat heavily. Within a few miles, he became delirious. He ranted and raved incoherently, going in and out of consciousness.

"I'll kill that bastard, Brady," he shouted. Then silence.

"That asshole...I'll kill him if I ever see him again."

I was really scared. I had no idea what was going on with him and didn't know what to do, other than to get him help as soon as I could. I told him to hang on and that we would soon be at the seminary. My words of encouragement seemed only to make things worse.

"Mike, don't take me there!" he shouted, above the noise of the rattling truck.

"I won't have those bastards looking after me...Don't take me there. I don't want to be anywhere near them."

"OK, Paddy, where do you want me to go?" I was the new kid on the block and was out of other options.

"Take me to Akwanga."

I knew roughly where the place was, having passed through it once, and also knew that a group of nuns had a hospital there. As I took the road through Keffi, I stopped briefly to let off Sammy, my cook, with a note telling the rector, Barney, what had happened and where I had gone.

I drove like a maniac, with Paddy going in and out of delirium. He continued ranting, raving, cursing, and sometimes just lapsed into complete silence. I was sick with worry and didn't know if I was doing the right thing. I was afraid he might die, and he was my partner, my friend. Fortunately, the road from Keffi to Akwanga was one of the few paved roads in the area, and I rapidly completed the forty miles.

The sisters knew right away what was wrong. He had malaria. They gave him an IV, and the effect was dramatic and wonderful. I knew he was OK and would fully recover, but it would clearly be some time before the doctor would release him. I was tremendously grateful to the sister in charge and the German nurse, Agnes, who took care of him.

"You must learn from this," she chided me as we were standing at the foot of his bed in a small side room at the hospital. "Always take your malaria tablets. People die from this every year."

"Thank you for all that you are doing for him," I replied, "and, yes, you don't have to convince me of how important it is."

"We intend to keep him here for about a week so he can get some rest. Why don't you come back then? He will be fine."

After I was told that he would recover, I took stock of what we both looked like! We hadn't shaved for a couple of days, hadn't had the time to shower, and were covered in fine red dust. I can only assume that we smelled the way we looked, but nobody said anything. Either they were used to folk showing up straight from the bush, or they were simply too polite to make any remark!

Unable to get another message to the seminary, I was besieged with questions when I returned. Everybody gathered in the sitting room, wanting to hear all of the details. I told them Paddy had malaria and that I would go back for him in a week's time. Barney was both irritated and concerned that we were exposing ourselves to this sort of thing by going on safari and that his worst fears, that we might not be able to keep our class schedules, were being realized. JP made his opinions clearly known in predictable fashion.

"You young priests think that you know it all," he admonished, shaking an accusatory finger at me. "If you get sick out here, it's all your own fault. You get what you deserve. If Paddy had taken proper precautions, he would never have gotten malaria in the first place. And now he has created additional work for all of us. Someone will have to cover his classes."

I was feeling very protective of Paddy, so I asked pointedly but knowingly, "And you JP, have you ever had malaria, have you never been sick in your twenty years out here?"

He glared at me angrily. "Some people are just too smart for their own breeches," he snapped back. And with that he stormed off outside.

Our kitchen was a small, free-standing building about fifty feet from the main house. A narrow path curved between the two structures, bordered by a low, well-grown hedge on either side. One day, the cook invited Paddy and me to see a deadly African Beauty Snake he had just killed; it was about three feet long with gold lines and a diamond pattern along its back. We were impressed. Then Paddy had an idea: this was a great opportunity to give JP his comeuppance and he asked me to participate.

It was just before lunch, and knowing that JP would be close by since he was responsible for all meals, Paddy placed the snake across the path

29

midway between the house and the kitchen. Standing on the kitchen steps, I shouted for him.

"JP, JP! Come quickly, JP!"

He appeared on the verandah.

"Come quickly! The cook has had an accident!" I put an air of concern into my voice. Rushing down the steps, he began to run towards the kitchen. As soon as he approached the curve in the path, Paddy shouted, "SNAKE!" just as JP was about to tread upon it. The man was visibly airborne for several seconds, landing on all fours, then scrambling on his hands and knees to escape. Meanwhile, we both broke out into uncontrollable laughter. Since we had made a fool of him, he was furious. He screamed at our stupidity and rushed into his bedroom. We both noticed that he came out wearing a clean pair of shorts. He never, ever forgave us.

True to the promise to move me into a parish as soon as possible, one evening a surprise visitor, Pete Clarke arrived with the news. He announced to the whole community that I was being reassigned as his assistant; I would be going to Igedde with him. He would first travel to Jos, the State capital, to purchase supplies and would pick me up on the way back.

I was thrilled with the news and had one week in which to hand over all my classes and get my loads prepared.

Pete was very much the life and soul of any party, a great raconteur who loved to sing and had that Irish penchant for telling jokes. He also enjoyed a whiskey. That evening as four of us were having a rowdy game of cards, JP, who had decided not to join us, complained that we were making too much noise. He said he had to get up early in the morning (as we all did)! I'm sure that we tried to be a little quieter, but about thirty minutes later he appeared again, and taking a supercilious schoolmasterish tone admonished us, "I hope you lot aren't going to sit here all night drinking."

Pete, who had been a classmate of JP's, tried to make a joke of it. So he quipped back, "Since you're here and you're in charge of the booze, why don't you find me another bottle of whiskey?"

It was the wrong thing to say. JP flew into a rage, calling us a "bunch of drunkards with no sense of priestly responsibility."

Barney remained quiet, probably having experienced this sort of outburst before, but clearly not knowing how to handle this particular situation. Jackie, with his usual, gentle manner, tried to be the peace maker.

"JP, why don't you go back to bed, and we will try to keep the noise level down?" For some reason unknown to us, but one that apparently went back to the distant past, JP suddenly attacked Pete.

"Clarke, I don't know why you came here. You're a drunkard with a well-known reputation. The next time you come, I hope I will be away, but in any case you should bring your own alcohol. You are a scandal-monger with no respect for authority; and you are responsible for creating negative factions in the diocese and almost preventing the election of the new bishop."

Paddy who had worked as Pete's assistant prior to his assignment at the seminary, was clearly bothered and angry at this outburst. Turning around in his chair to better face him, he shouted, "JP, that was uncalled for. For God's sake, cut it out and go back to bed."

But now Pete, too, was furious. Throwing his cards on the table, he jumped to his feet and pointed a finger right into JP's face. "I have never been so insulted in my life. And JP, you are just a sterile faggot, who should never have been ordained."

I was too shocked to say anything. I had nothing to say anyway. It all felt so uncomfortable for me, seeing priests abuse each other like this. In my own naïve mind, I somehow held a mental separation between student life and that of an ordained minister. We said and did things as students that were not right, but I just never imagined that such an exchange could take place between priests, and especially a group that claimed to be a "brotherhood."

Even though it was well past midnight, Pete wanted to leave right away. "I've had enough of this fucking place," he said. "I should never have come here. This was sure to happen one way or another. I will not stay another night under the same roof as JP. It's not too late to go to Akwanga for the night."

The five of us responded almost as one voice. "Absolutely not, it is far too dangerous, Pete, and you know it."

Barney suggested that too much had been said for one night, and that we all turn in.

In the morning, before anyone was up, I heard a truck leaving the compound. It was Pete's. He returned a week later to pick me up, but he wouldn't stay for lunch, and once my cases were loaded, we took off for my new home.

He left a bottle of whiskey with Barney, and asked him to give it to JP to make up for what he had drunk. Barney refused, so it was left sitting on the kitchen table. JP didn't come out of his room to greet Pete or to see me off. I had never before witnessed two mature priests behaving with so much embitterment. The whole incident really disturbed me. I was still a rookie, and was easily shocked at how human, and sometimes immature, some of my brother priests were. I was particularly bothered since Pete was now my new pastor.

Nine months later I visited the seminary and many changes had taken place. Barney was still the rector and as kind and gentle as ever. We walked together up and down the driveway, enjoying the shade of the avenue of trees in full bloom, while he gave me the latest news.

"JP's behavior was more and more bizarre, as he became increasingly discontented with the reforms in the Catholic Church. We had to send him home, and the last I heard was that he had left the Order, and was searching out a group that was devoted to maintaining the use of Latin in the Church"

"Well," I said, "I am not surprised at all."

"Dennis never came back to Keffi. He has been appointed to take charge of translating catechisms and liturgical texts into native languages and works in the new center in Gboko. I've heard that he is very good at it, and is very happy."

"And how is Pete?" Barney asked.

"Wow, Barney," I exclaimed, and suddenly stopping to face him. "I'm so surprised you haven't heard."

It all seemed so long ago now, but his question quickly brought back the memories of that Sunday evening as Pete and I were sitting out on the patio after a long day's work, enjoying each other's company and catching up on the business of the day.

"Mike," Pete said, "I have something very difficult to share with you."

"That's OK, Pete, I can handle it," I replied half jokingly.

"But this is serious, Mike, and I want you to listen very carefully."

"Then please tell me," I urged.

"Mike, you don't know this, but the new Bishop and I have never gotten along. In fact, there have been years of real conflict. I've known him too long, ever since we were in the seminary together, and I'm not prepared to work under him as Bishop. I'm leaving Nigeria for good. I won't give you the sordid details; you are new to the diocese and I don't wish in any way to prejudice you." He took a long drink from his beer glass, all the while starring out towards the hills as if searching for something, his suntanned face creased with a deep frown.

I was speechless. "What can I say, Pete?" All of sudden the bottom had dropped out of my world. I was growing to admire this man as a fine human being. He was also a wonderful pastor, and I loved the way he was coaching me in my ministry. But he was not done yet.

"Mike, you also need to know that when I get back to Ireland, I will also be leaving the Order."

"And when will all this happen, Pete?" I stammered, struggling to keep back my tears.

"I would like you to take me to the airport the day after tomorrow. We will go to Aliade first so I can say goodbye to Jack, and then on to Jos by Wednesday."

So quickly, I thought; it was all too quick.

I slept very little that night or for that matter the next night as well. I functioned as if in a fog with so many thoughts and concerns going through my mind. If Pete was leaving, then who would be next? That concern troubled me a great deal. And what about me, I asked myself selfishly, who would be my new boss, how would I cope? I could manage this huge parish on my own for a while, but it was too much for one man, and in any case, I was smart enough to know that I still had lots to learn about life and ministry in a bush parish.

CHAPTER 3

Initiation

MONSOON SEASON. A red sky at dawn faded when the rain came. It began as a gray curtain drifting across the savannah, but gale-force winds soon drove it in darkening sheets. Palm trees whipsawed side to side, shaking their heads in disapproval. The noise on the tin roof was deafening. Huge flashes of lightning accompanied by incessant thunder reverberated off the nearby Igedde hills and illuminated the compound. It lasted all day.

Inside my rain-lashed home, it was warm and snug. Being housebound gave me the opportunity to balance my accounts, complete my logs and clean up my office, but by evening time, I was satisfied and tired and I needed to relax. A quick shower and a meal helped, but I was restless. I tried reading, but couldn't focus. The isolation of the past four months, living on my own in such a remote area with no partner even to talk to, was now beginning to bother me. Loneliness was setting in. Perhaps I could keep the demons at bay by writing home. It had been too long since I had brought family and friends up to date on my latest adventures.

I recalled that typical dark, damp, cold and foggy Liverpool winter evening when I boarded the SS Aureol on my journey to Africa, not knowing when I would return. As I waved to my parents on the quayside far below, I wondered if I would ever see them again. Each family member had stoically tried not to show emotion. My parents looked so small, frail, and sad, my mother in tears. As the ship pulled away from the dock, I watched them shrink in size until they were swallowed up in the mist, as if some giant had cast his grey cloak over them.

I was filled with mixed feelings, but at that moment a deep sadness prevailed. After all, here I was a newly ordained, twenty-six-year old priest, a member of a French Religious Missionary Order, *Les Peres du Saint Esprit*, better known in the United States as *Holy Ghost Fathers* or *Spiritans*, setting out for my life's work. It would be in Nigeria, the "white man's grave," which was in a state of civil war. In spite of reassurances, there were many unknowns.

As the ship turned into the main channel and the lights of the city receded, my feelings changed. The constant pulsing of the huge turbines, the great power of their thrust and the ship's gentle pitch and roll, created in me the thrill and excitement of adventure. I had never before sailed on a ship this large.

I was in my cabin which I was sharing with a young water engineer from Wales, and we had hardly had time to introduce ourselves, when an alarm bell sounded. Over the speaker system a boat drill was announced. Like everyone else, I immediately tried to find my way through what seemed to be a maze of stairways, corridors, and heavy doors. Gradually, I found myself with a large group of strangers, fighting the wind, rain, and spray on the boat deck. The sea was inky black save for some bobbing lights in the distance, which I took to be another, smaller ship. Trying to make conversation was almost impossible because of the wind. Suddenly, a voice with a strong Liverpool accent sounded.

"Well, then, lets 'ave a look at you."

We all turned to face this apparition that seemed to have materialized out of nowhere. A short stocky man, buried in a navy-blue pea coat with its collar turned up, wearing an officer's cap, bull-horn in hand, was smiling at us. "'Ave you all got a life jacket? If not, go back and get it."

It appeared we all had achieved that much.

"Well, then, what are you waiting for? Put it on. I need to inspect you."

The humor in this man's voice was obvious. We formed ourselves into two lines as we all struggled in the wind to sort out this unfamiliar piece of equipment. The officer talked and joked non-stop, as he gently helped some older folks with their life jackets. I had fastened mine incorrectly, snagging a long loop that was attached to the collar of the vest. When he saw what I had done, he said, "Eh, Padre, don't do that. I need that loop so I can pull you out of the water when the ship goes down."

Up to that moment, I hadn't for one-second thought about that being a real possibility!

At Freetown, Sierra Leone, many local passengers came on board, and lodged under a canvas awning set up over the forward deck. I had struck up a friendship with a nun, Sister Enya, who was a medical doctor and had spent twelve years in Nigeria. One evening as we were leaning over the railing of the upper deck, enjoying the sunset and taking in all the activity down below, a man sitting with a large group of people got up, suddenly walked to the side of the ship, unzipped his shorts, and peed out to sea. While not exactly shocked, I was embarrassed for the nun and wasn't sure what to say. She, however, didn't bat an eyelid and without even turning away said, "Father Michael there are some things you see, that tell you without a doubt you are back in Africa!"

The memories and experiences of landing in Lagos, the principal port of Nigeria, are etched forever in my memory. Before my passport, visas, and work permit were stamped, a young immigration officer asked, "How much money are you bringing into the country?"

"I have almost nothing," I nervously replied, "just a few coins and some traveler's checks. I am a Catholic priest and missionary, not a businessman."

"Then how much will you pay me?" he asked, waiting expectantly, all the while leafing through my passport and papers.

I had no idea what he meant, so I repeated that it was all I had since it was illegal to bring Nigerian currency into the country.

Clearly irritated with me, he snapped, "Empty out all of your pockets."

Very conscious of all the military personnel and police walking around carrying automatic weapons, I began to feel quite nervous. I also felt very alone. Nobody had told me to expect this situation, nor how to deal with it if it did arise. My consternation and helplessness must have shown, because after looking at what must have been small pickings for him, he brusquely and suddenly stamped my papers, ordering me with a dismissive wave of the hand to move on.

My experience in the cavernous, baggage hall was not much better. I searched for the aisle with the letter B and then for my boxes. There should have been four, but now there were six, my name clearly stenciled in bold letters on each one! There were two huge crates that I didn't recognize. It turned out that they were for another priest who knew me; he'd had them sent directly to the ship. Apparently, this was the customary way of getting mission supplies not available in Nigeria. He had, however, not only failed to inform me, but I also had no idea what was inside them.

Surrounded by a sweating, shouting, heaving mass of people again, I didn't know what to do next. My basic instructions from England did not cover this situation. All I'd been told was that a priest would meet me and take me and my baggage to some place in Lagos! From there, I'd be given a ride upcountry to Makurdi. I saw people having their crates opened by personnel in khaki uniforms. I approached a gray haired, kind-looking Nigerian passenger dressed in very colorful robes and asked about the process.

"You must get hold of one of these gentlemen," he indicated, pointing to men dressed in khaki and carrying small tool boxes. "They are carpenters. Have one of them open your crates, and then go looking for a customs officer who will clear them. They are the people wearing green caps. Afterwards you will need another carpenter who will close up your crates again."

It was hopeless. There were not enough people to open the crates and no order to the whole thing. I approached several workers, asking them to come and open my boxes. Each one carefully and expectantly looked me over and said "yes," they would come when they had finished with the person they were currently helping. Nobody showed up. I tried three or four more times, and still nobody came. Slowly the huge hall began to empty. The ship had docked at nine o' clock, and by now it was almost three in the afternoon. The temperature and humidity were unbearable. The silent ceiling fans high up in the rafters looked like they would disintegrate if they had operated. They did not, and even if they had, they would have made little impact on the oppressive heat. I felt helpless and nervous and ready to throw up, for I had had nothing to eat or drink since very early morning. I was the only white person left and was approached by a very tall, overweight and bearded senior customs officer wearing a uniform clearly several sizes too small. In spite of my situation, I could not help noticing the sweat stains all around his collar and even larger ones under his armpits. He constantly mopped his dripping brow with a large khaki handkerchief.

"Why haven't you opened your crates?" he bellowed.

"I am a Catholic priest, and my boxes contain only materials for the missions, but I haven't been able to get anybody to help me," I stammered.

"Then you will have to pay a carpenter to open them."

"I'm willing to pay," I said, "but I can't find a carpenter. I was told that it was illegal to bring Nigerian currency into the country, but I do have some travelers' checks."

For one split second I thought I saw his eyes flicker and his face soften slightly, as if in anticipation of aiding another helpless victim.

"Then give me some," he said.

I fumbled with my wallet, as a sweaty hand extended itself from a ludicrously short sleeve.

"How much should I pay the carpenter?" I asked.

"Don't worry," he said, "I'll take care of everything."

I only had English ten-pound travelers checks, and after detaching one was about to write on it.

"Don't do that," he said brusquely and snatched the check from my hand. "Give it to me. There is no need to write anything." After slowly and carefully looking it over, he said in a tone indicating perhaps that I had somehow insulted him, "Give me another one."

I passed him a second check, my hand shaking. He immediately summoned a man dressed in khaki who was rushing by.

"You there, come here at once," he bellowed, gesticulating with his hand in the direction of my boxes.

The man suddenly stopped dead in his tracks.

"Yes, sir!"

"Open these immediately!" he said, tapping one with his hand. "This man is important and you have kept him waiting."

I breathed a silent prayer that he had selected one of my own crates, since I knew what was in it. The officer gave a cursory look inside, asked me what else I had, and without even listening or looking at anything, told the man to close up the crate. He then chalk-marked all the crates, and told me I could go. There was nothing to declare. It had all taken place in less than five minutes! I didn't want to change my luck and spoil my chances of getting out of there, but I needed to know what to do next, and was about to ask the officer to help me when I heard my name called. A well-dressed, young black man about twenty years old had entered into the hall, and was looking around and shouting,

"Father Barrington! Father Barrington!"

I waved frantically until he saw me. He approached, running, and introduced himself.

"My name is Emmanuel, and I work for Father Malcolm, the priest in charge of Catholic Relief Services in Lagos. He apologizes for not meeting you and sent me instead. However, I've been stuck for hours in traffic. I'm sorry I'm so late."

I can't ever recall being so happy to see a total stranger. Within minutes he had taken charge and spoken to the officer in his native language (I learned later that it was Yoruba); more money changed hands, and several porters came running, took all the crates, and quickly loaded them onto Emmanuel's truck.

The chaotic drive across the city in almost unbearable heat and humidity, in a truck with no air conditioning, meant we had to keep the windows down. Strange smells of smog, exhaust fumes, open sewers and rotting vegetation assaulted my nostrils. In addition, the traffic's deafening noise made it practically impossible to converse. None of that seemed to matter because I was just relieved to be out of the customs shed. Emmanuel spoke excellent English, and when I related what had transpired in Immigration and Customs, he burst out laughing.

"You should have given the men a 'dash,' and they would have taken care of you right away."

"A 'dash'?" I queried.

"A 'dash' is simply a tip you give before you get the service," he explained. "Welcome to Nigeria. You must learn it quickly if you want to get anything done in this country, and it is good to know that sometimes you will give a 'dash' beforehand, and a 'dash' afterwards as well,"

"But why"? I asked innocently.

"Well, you have to judge each situation. A 'dash' beforehand can sometimes be called an incentive to get service, and the second 'dash' is the tip for the service given."

It began to make sense now why I had been ignored, and why things had begun to move only after I had given up my travelers' checks.

"You took charge so easily…"

"Because I gave a 'dash' to the customs officer."

"But I had already paid him twenty pounds to help me."

"Yes, but that was for you. I was new business for him."

"Then what about the porters?" I asked.

"There is a very definite hierarchy in every place, especially in government offices. The porters were given something by the officer and expected that I would give them a 'dash' anyway."

This was lesson number one in learning to survive and do business in Nigeria!

As he negotiated a turbulent sea of horn blowing, smoke belching, colorfully painted, overloaded and almost wrecked vehicles that seemed to have little or no order to it, he kept up a non-stop litany of his version of Nigerian culture.

"When driving, if you see an outstretched arm waving up and down out of the car in front of you, he is not signaling. It simply means the window is open. If a pig or a goat runs out of the bush in front of you, wait for a second one to follow. The length of any Nigerian speech depends upon the strength of the speaker's legs. On the seventh day while God rested, the Nigerians invented noise."

I was amazed at his repertoire. It gushed out like a sudden break in a major water main. With one hand firmly and permanently pressing the horn, the other spinning the wheel like a top, he nonchalantly squeezed the truck in and out of the jam-packed lanes.

"When a Nigerian prepares a meal, it is always in excess in anticipation that someone else will drop by," he emphasized, nodding his head in agreement with himself. "It is very bad etiquette to prepare a meal just for yourself; all foreigners are held personally responsible for their governments at home; when you call a Nigerian to come to you immediately, he will say 'I'm coming,' but in fact he means, 'I will come just as soon as I can,' and that could take ages."

I would have liked to hear more, but all of a sudden he swung the truck hard over to the left of the road, and with one wheel on the dirt sidewalk, turned into a one-way street. I was petrified.

"Didn't I see a sign indicating that this is a one-way street?" which was obvious since it was full of traffic.

"Yes, of course," he shouted laughingly.

"And aren't we traveling down it the wrong way?"

"Yes, but it does not matter. It is a shortcut to your apartment where you will be met by a Father from Makurdi. There are so few traffic cops in Lagos that there is little chance of being caught, so we do this all the time."

The apartment was air-conditioned and it felt really wonderful to escape the heat and humidity. I would have liked to spend more time with Emmanuel, but he had other business to attend to. He did have time for a glass of beer, and in the few minutes we spent together, once he had arranged for my crates to be brought in, he told me that he was in his final year at the University of Lagos. He was a literature major, and hoped one day to be a feature writer for a major newspaper or magazine.

"Jobs like that are very hard to find," he said, "so I will probably end up teaching. Right now I am working part time for Father Malcolm, and I concentrate on making sure that emergency relief supplies that come into the port, mainly from Ireland and the USA, go where they are supposed to go. Pilfering is a real problem, coupled with bribery at every level. But I do need to go," he said, standing up and offering me his hand. "It was a pleasure meeting you, Father Michael. Welcome to Nigeria."

"Thank you too: you have been a great help," I said, meaning every word of it. "Please give my best wishes and thanks to Father Malcolm."

I had known Ron Cammack in college and we had become good friends. It was great to see him again. Although he was a few years older than me, we had continued to write to each other once he left for Nigeria, and I was excited to see where he was working. He came into the apartment just as I was coming out of the shower. He had aged, but he was still the tall, well-built, nicely dressed person I remembered, though now he wore a white shirt, shorts, and knee-length socks. His bushy, wavy hair spilled out from under a new looking bush hat which he wore at a jaunty angle, looking for all the world like some big game hunter. He told me he had just purchased it and would like me to get one the next day. It turned out that the two mysterious crates were his. We re-connected very quickly. He wanted news from the UK, and I wanted a crash course on life in the tropics. The Bishop of Makurdi had asked him to meet me and drive me up north.

We had dinner at the stylish Hamdala hotel. The beers were ice-cold and served by impeccably dressed waiters. Ron had arranged to meet some business people at the hotel, since he was negotiating the purchase of tires that could be used on both pick-up trucks and Land Rovers, apparently they were very scarce. Other than seeing a few army officers in full uniform, we could have been a million miles away from a country locked in a horrible civil war. At this point it was only a few months old, but the expectation was that it would go on for some time and be a bloody affair.

Ron was helpful to me and made sure I bought everything I might need: bush hat, knee-length white socks, etc., all items that could not be obtained upcountry. He took me to a mission tailor where I was measured for a half-dozen, white cassocks. From there we went to an older part of town where I had my photograph taken in the street with an incredible home-made wooden camera. The photos were developed on the spot, and the results were at least recognizable. I would need one of them for my driver's license.

At the Post Office we saw long lines of people waiting. There were street vendors, beggars, and hustlers everywhere. Heavily armed police and military personnel were also very much in evidence. Ron went up to a person wearing a Nigerian Post Office uniform who was seated at a desk inside the main door.

"Can you please tell me where I can get a driver's license?" he enquired.

"I'm sorry," said the man. "I don't give out that kind of information; I only deal with identity cards. You will need to ask the messengers." He pointed to a group of youths leaning against the wall outside.

I learned from Ron that he was not being rude. The official probably knew the answer but was just being bureaucratic, the hallmark of Nigerian civil service that was really a left-over from the British administration. As we approached the group, four or five young men rushed towards us, each asking if we needed stamps, passport forms and so on.

"I need somebody to help me get a driving license for this Father," Ron announced. "Who can take care of it quickly?"

The group surged forward.

"Let me do it," each one cried, but familiar with this routine, Ron opted for a tall, articulate and strong-looking young man.

"He is a priest from England, and he does not have a Nigerian driving license."

"It is not a problem," the youth replied. "Does he have the photos?"

"Yes," said Ron, turning towards me and extending his hand.

"Then let me have them. I will do everything for you. I will fill out all your forms, sign them, and return with the license. Please give me the money."

Ron then nodded to me and said, "Give him the money, Mike, his 'dash' and your English license."

"But I don't have any Nigerian money; I only have travelers' checks."

"It doesn't matter to these guys. What bills do you have?"

Once again I produced my travelers' checks, and pointed to a ten pound check. "Give him that," Ron said.

Again without either signing or dating it, I handed a check over to the messenger.

The man appeared delighted. I felt very unsure about the whole transaction and was especially concerned with handing over one of my few pieces of ID to a total stranger. My fears were unfounded. The young man re-appeared after only about fifteen minutes with a shiny new red driver's license. I asked Ron how he could get a license in my name since I hadn't taken a driver's test. How had he short-circuited the long lines?

"Because he knows how to use the 'dash'; the other people are in line because they don't want to give one!"

Will I ever be able to get used to this system? I thought. Intellectually I understand the explanation I have been given, and admire the way Ron handles everything, but to me it's as if I am giving a bribe. I am getting what I want, but I feel that in some way I am compromising my moral values. I need to pray about this.

Our journey north was in Ron's Peugeot 403 pickup, the standard truck for most missions, which was loaded way over capacity. Getting out of Lagos was a harrowing experience, and a warning of what was in front of us. There were heavily armed military check points and separate police check points every few miles in some places. As we moved farther north and east, they increased in number. Before we reached our destination, the town of Makurdi eight hundred miles away, we would have stopped at more than thirty of them, each one a difficult and nerve-wracking experience.

The morning before we were ready to leave, we heard some disconcerting news on the radio. A news announcer mis-read the script and spoke about the many "missionaries" who were fighting with Biafra, the breakaway rebel state. He obviously should have read "mercenaries!" It made us very jittery, and each time we were stopped Ron had a hard time explaining why we were carrying so many boxes, and especially the tires. He had suggested it might help if we both traveled wearing our white robes so that we could be clearly identified as priests, but it did nothing to reduce my anxiety. I was a sweaty bag of nerves the whole time we were on the road.

Benin City was on the main road leading to the war zone, and there was a heavy military presence everywhere. Thousands of soldiers were marching and chanting in unison; long lines of army trucks took up most of the roads, some pulling heavy weapons. All traffic was controlled by military police. Before we headed to the cathedral parish house where we would spend the night, Ron drove into the suburbs where the houses were more dilapidated and crowded together, resembling a shanty town.

"Where are we heading?" I asked once we left the town center.

"I am going to get some essential medical supplies. They are unavailable in our area, and I know a couple of French Canadian nuns who run a clinic near here. They have helped me out in the past."

He turned off the dirt road onto an even narrower road that wound its way up a steep incline through a large banana plantation. He corrected me as I commented on the size of the fruit.

"Those are not bananas, Mike, they are plantains," he laughed, and since I had never even heard the name previously, he proceeded to give me a quick education as to their usefulness.

We pulled up in front of a neat, relatively small square building that was painted white with blue shutters and trim. Next to it a group of women were sitting outside on benches that were set out in neat rows under a long, grass-roofed, open-sided shelter.

"So this is a maternity clinic," I said.

"Yes, it is," he responded, "but it also operates as a general purpose clinic since there is no other medical center in this area."

I was glad to get out of the truck and stretch my aching back. We had been driving continuously for five hours, stopping only to pick up gas. This was just another item in my acculturation: "never drive past a gas station, always take advantage and fill up since there is a strong possibility of the next one being closed and empty." It was only then that I realized just what a sight we looked. Our once white cassocks were now deeply soiled and stained by the red laterite dust, especially where we had been sweating.

A woman, who had heard our truck arrive, suddenly appeared at the screen door.

"Come on in," she called out recognizing that we were priests, and I suppose, seeing our load of equipment guessing that we were heading for the bush.

"I'm Sister Imelda," she announced in a strong Irish brogue. "I am the nurse in charge here." She held out her hand to both of us. "Come on in and sit down; you both look tired. How can I help you? I am about to close up."

"I called here about ten days ago," Ron said, "and spoke to Sister Jeanne Luc, a French Canadian nun. I asked her to put together a box of medical supplies for me; I told her I would collect it on my return. I've been to Lagos to get supplies and pick up this newly arrived priest."

"Oh, so you are the one," she responded, a sign of recognition spreading over her face. "I have the box right here; sister told me about it. It's quite heavy, so let me get one of my staff to carry it out for you."

"Adam," she called through an open door addressing a young man in what was obviously a small laboratory. "Would you kindly help Father with this box?"

She followed us out to the truck and stood while we secured it.

"Would you like a cold drink?" she asked, turning as if she already knew the answer and walking over to a house next door to the clinic. It was obviously the convent. As we climbed the steps behind her, I could not help but notice that she had beautifully tanned legs.

"I would have liked to invite you to a late lunch," she said in an apologetic tone, "but I don't have a cook. He is home sick and I just have a sandwich which I fixed this morning."

"Please don't worry about us," Ron interjected quickly. "We'll head over to the central mission house downtown once we're finished here. Do you mind if I smoke?" he asked.

A young woman who looked like a schoolgirl magically appeared unannounced, carrying a tray with glasses, water, and couple of beers. She silently placed it on the low table in front of us.

"Thank you, Beatrice," Imelda said gently.

And then, turning to Ron, "Yes, you may smoke," she said, "and you might hand me one also, if you don't mind. It will save me going to my room."

He stood up, held the packet so she could help herself, then leaned over and offered her a light.

"We'll be spending the night downtown," he announced. "You must be new here. I met Francine on my last visit and Jeanne Luc has been a friend for several years. They told me they were the only ones here."

There was a long pause as she took a long draw on her cigarette, "Something terrible has happened here, Fathers," she announced in almost a whisper, "something really shocking. I am here because Sister Jeanne Luc is not well."

It was only then that I noticed her face. It was quite young. She cannot have been more than thirty-five years old and she was very pretty. But she had very red, tired eyes and it was obvious she had been crying. The tiredness in her face reflected more than fatigue; it was filled with a deep sadness.

After putting her glass down, she continued, "Jeanne Luc is here and I will ask her if she will see you, Ron."

And with that she got up and vanished down a hallway, reappearing just a few seconds later.

"Yes, it is ok. You will see the open door on the left hand side."

It wasn't until we were back in the truck that I heard the full story. Sister Francine was in town trying to arrange a flight back to Canada for Jeanne Luc. Apparently Jeanne was returning from visiting a bush clinic two days ago and ran into a small military patrol. They beat up her driver, did the same to her, and then gang raped her. She was in pretty bad shape.

I was aghast. My God, I thought, this is exactly what happened in the Congo. Many of the nuns were raped, became pregnant and eventually left their Religious Orders. The Pope later allowed nuns, if they were in immediate danger, to use birth control pills which caused quite a furor in certain Catholic

circles. But out here? I had never given it a thought. How horrible! This poor
nun would be traumatized for the rest of her life.

"Hopefully they will have her out of here tomorrow," Ron said. "At least the military has persuaded the air force to get her to Lagos. Francine should be back later this afternoon with her air ticket. Only time will tell if she is pregnant or not. And Mike when we get to the mission house, let's just keep our ears open and mouths shut. I really liked Jeanne Luc, but I probably will never see her again."

Back on the road, the main bridge over the Niger River leading into Onitsha had been blown up, so we had to drive much further north in order to cross by ferry at Lokoja, a long, bumpy detour of a couple of hundred miles. Even so, the ferry was under strict military control, and there was no guarantee that we would be allowed to cross.

Hundreds of civilian vehicles were waiting in line, in addition to seemingly miles of military trucks and weaponry. Heavily armed soldiers seemed to be everywhere, milling around, eating, sleeping, and playing loud music. I thought we'd be stranded here for days until our turn came. Ron, however, nonchalantly drove past them and approached the military check point directly. I wondered frankly what he was doing and I was extremely nervous. The shabbily dressed guards at the barrier looked to be about fifteen years old, and one of them, full of his own importance, was irate that we'd apparently jumped the queue. He wouldn't let us pass until we had allowed him to see all of our boxes, pointing his gun at us in a threatening manner the whole time. Ron, however, knew the system well.

"Sergeant," he said (the man was only a private), "I'm sure you can take us to the Commander of the Ferry. I have business that concerns his wife." The flattery and the intimation of something important worked immediately.

"Yes, sir, follow me," he snapped, and led us on foot down a narrow path through a maze of military tents, mountains of discarded boxes, bottles and garbage, eventually ending on the river bank.

Seated on a home-made deck chair under a makeshift awning of palm fronds, was a jovial looking military officer, a bottle of beer in his hand, his feet resting on an up-turned ammunition case, the top buttons of his sweaty uniform jacket undone. Seeing us approaching, his face broke out into an obvious smile of recognition. Close up I noticed that his face, especially his cheeks, were heavily scarred with tribal markings.

"Ah, so the Reverend Father has returned," he remarked, easing himself out of his chair and shaking the dust from his trousers. "I hope that you have had a successful journey."

"Captain Adekunle, this is the new Father from England I told you about," Ron explained, pointing in my direction, "and he is very concerned about being able to cross the river safely today."

"You are welcome, Father," he said, extending me his hand. "Welcome to Nigeria. And how is Sandhurst? I spent six months there at the military academy."

Not even knowing where Sandhurst was and unsure if our crossing depended somewhat on my response, I hesitated momentarily. Ron quickly rescued me. Wiping the sweat off his forehead with the brim of his bush hat, he announced, "I have a special gift for your wife. I trust that her pregnancy is progressing well so I have brought a case of Guinness for her." So this was the bait, I thought. I had wondered why he had bought it in Lagos!

Positively beaming, the commander squeezed Ron's hand again and again. "Let me tell you that I will take you over the river myself immediately without any problem. I will personally supervise your crossing. You have my word."

I was not sure what value his word would have been if the Biafrans had started shelling us, though I was assured that the front lines were many miles away.

"But where is your truck?" he asked Ron, looking around, suddenly realizing that we had arrived on foot.

Speaking calmly but purposefully, Ron replied, "I had to leave it at the barrier since your men have not yet given us clearance." It was only at that moment I realized what a wonderful act Ron had put on. One could almost see what was coming next. The young soldier was still standing at attention, awaiting further instructions.

Turning to him, the Captain emitted what initially sounded like a low growl but then erupted into an apoplectic outburst.

"You stupid, damn, bloody fool!" the Captain bellowed at the unfortunate man, shaking a finger in his face. "You prevent my good friend the Reverend Father from bringing his gift to me? You are a very foolish, ignorant bushman. Yes, you are from deep in the bush. How dare you insult my friends?" (I later learned that this was a criticism that no Nigerian would want to hear.) Practically shoving him forward, the Captain ordered him, "Go and let the Fathers pass immediately. I will punish you later."

This "dash" appeared to have been very well accepted, and surrounded by army jeeps and personnel carriers, we were slowly transported across the Niger. The barge itself was so underpowered that the pilot had to take it against the current close to the river bank for about a half a mile, before actually turning into the main stream heading out towards the other side. The Commander even allowed me to take photographs on the actual ferry, which surprised me since we were in an active military zone where cameras were expressly forbidden.

I wandered around the ferry and spoke with a shabbily dressed soldier carrying an automatic rifle covered with mud. The rifle bore was caked with red dirt, but he didn't seem to mind. I couldn't help thinking that I wouldn't want to be around him if he had to use it, and discreetly but purposefully moved to the other side of the barge.

The sight, size, and force of the river left me with a feeling of awe. It was far bigger than anything I had seen or experienced in Europe. Images of Victorian African explorers whose books I had devoured as a kid and who had fired my imagination flashed through my mind: Burton, Stanley, Baker, Livingstone, Mungo Park. For one brief moment, in spite of all the attendant circumstances, Africa was a very romantic place and seeing the Niger was almost like meeting an old childhood friend. I wanted to trail my hand in the river just to feel its coolness.

My German shepherd, Rascal, gently licking my fingers broke my reverie. For a few seconds I was disoriented and it took me a moment to realize where I was. It was now dark outside and my unfinished letter now had a black scrawl across one corner. So much had happened in the sixteen months I had been in Nigeria. I realized that my life had changed forever. I also realized that it was very late and I was dead tired.

CHAPTER 4

Affection

Her name was Eugenia. How she got that name I will never know, but it suited her. She was a small, beautiful twelve-year-old schoolgirl with a disarming smile. Unlike most of her people, she was very light-skinned. Her well worn, but clean, green-and-white uniform was stretched tight as her growing body struggled with its constraints.

I first met her in class when I was doing my usual rounds at the local grade school, and I'd made a remark about her intricate braids. I soon discovered that she was extremely bright. A few days after our first meeting, she came over to the mission house on her way home. The house was set back about fifty yards from the narrow path leading to the main village; it was on the same compound as the school. Frequently when I was in my office, people would wave as they passed, or shout a greeting.

I could see Eugenia approaching, singing to herself, swinging her books tied together with a string and clutching a small bag which contained her writing materials. She sat down on the verandah floor outside of my open office door, watching me work. The larger of my two dogs, Roco, sauntered over, flopped down beside her, allowing her to play with his ears. He was not usually that friendly.

"Hi Eugenia, how are you today? Is there something I can do for you?"

"No thank you, Barrington," she replied, her focus remaining on the dog.

I continued working for a few minutes, engrossed in trying to balance my accounts when she broke the silence.

"Barrington, excuse me please, but do you have a book I can read? I want to learn more things and I have finished all my school books."

"Well, that's a great request, Eugenia," I said pushing my chair back and walking towards her. "I do have some books, but I wonder if they are the kind that you would want. Come in and we can take a look at them together."

I had quite a collection of books in the office, but none for kids. I did have a selection of African Writers Series books that I personally found fascinating. I pulled out *Things Fall Apart* by Chinu Achebe, a Nigerian writer, recounting the story of a village "big man" who gets his comeuppance.

"Do you want to give this one a try? You might like the story."

"If you liked it, Barrington, then perhaps I will," she answered trustingly.

"Then you can borrow it. If you don't like it we will try something else. In any case, you can always come here and ask me for help."

From that day Eugenia would frequently come to the mission house with a couple of friends after classes, just to sit and visit or ask me for another book to read. She had an impish sense of humor and a quick inquisitive mind. She also had a somewhat deformed right foot that forced her to walk with a slight limp.

I learned from the headmaster that this young girl was also industrious, determined, and responsible well beyond her years. Since she was one of only two people in her village who could read — the other was her elder brother — she had started evening classes in her father's compound twice a week, teaching adults. At every class, she asked each person for a penny that she put towards buying her own uniform and class materials.

"Barrington," she called to me one day after school as she was sitting with her best friend Teresa, dangling their legs over the edge of the verandah shaded by the huge mango tree, "Will you take me to England with you so I can go to a big school? I would like to become a doctor." It was siesta time, and the heat was so oppressive that I could not rest. I was sitting at my desk with the doors and windows wide open, trying to catch what little movement of air there was, and she must have seen that I was not concentrating on my work.

"Well, it's far, far away, and you would miss your own people," I replied, walking out and squatting down between the girls. It felt a little cooler outside even though the cement was warm to the touch. Roco loped over from the shade under my truck where he had been sleeping, flopped down between us, and nuzzled up to the two girls. Then she coyly turned her head, looking at me in a disarming way with just the hint of a smile, with something between impishness and genuine curiosity.

"But you are a rich man," she continued. "You can bring all of my family too."

"What do you mean rich?" I laughed.

"Well, you have a truck and a big stone house, and if you get a bad sickness, you can go home to find a doctor."

For a moment I was not sure just how to respond; she had taken me completely unawares. "You're right," I replied, searching for the appropriate thing to say. "I do have a nice house, but it doesn't belong to me. I'm only using it as long as I work in Igedde. And yes, priests do get sent to England if they are very sick, but that's because they are not as strong as you and your people."

"But Barrington, we want you stay for a long, long time," she declared. "Our people like you. I do not want you to get sick, but if it comes, you must stay and I will help take care of you."

I was touched by her childlike simplicity and obvious affection. I wanted to reply with something witty, but I was too slow.

"Barrington, why don't you have a wife?" Eugenia ventured. "She could take care of you."

"Eugenia, you know that priests do not marry. You learned that in school. None of the other priests that have lived here in the mission have been married."

"Yes, but all the priests who have been here were old and you are young. There are many women here who would be a good wife for you. If you married one you would stay here and our people would be very happy." She fidgeted with some loose threads on the frayed edge of her dress, not looking me in the eyes for once. "Do you not want to be married; do you not want children of your own?"

I was taken aback, and getting more uncomfortable by the moment. This was not the playful Eugenia who laughed and joked with me. Her questions were not only prying; they were tapping into something very deep within me. How could I explain to her that at one level I was very satisfied with my life as a celibate priest, and that marriage had never been an option for me? Or how could I tell her that sometimes I ached to have a wife and children? Not knowing which was the greater truth, silenced me. I was a young priest with the highest of ideals; I could not afford to have these kinds of thoughts, I told myself. There was no room in my life for any ambiguity in this regard. In my silence, I suddenly became acutely aware of the loud twittering of the weaver birds in the tree close by.

Finally, I resorted to a convenient answer. "Priests don't marry so that they can give all their attention to God's work and to the people in each parish."

"But a good wife would help you do that," Eugenia quickly retorted. "That's what wives do. They support their husbands."

"It's very hot out here," I sighed, eager to change the subject. "Would you like a cold fruit juice?"

"Yes, please," the girls responded in unison.

"Then let's go inside and see what we can find."

It took just a couple of minutes to fix the drinks. As we walked back to the shade of the verandah, Eugenia took her friend's hand, and said brightly, "Barrington, you are learning our language well, and there are many women in our father's compound who would be good for you." With that mischievous twinkle in her eye that I knew so well, she added, "Should we talk to him for you?"

I chuckled, deeply embarrassed. "No, don't do that. It would cost me too much money in dowry." I sipped my drink, wondering what was coming next. But while Eugenia was silent, I decided to turn the tables. "And what about you, will you get married soon?" I asked.

"Oh no," she responded immediately, "I have already told you that I want to be a doctor. I want to go to college. My father wanted to promise me to his brother in Ihigile, but I told him that I must finish my education first. He now understands that I will be worth much more money once I have been to college."

There she goes again, I thought to myself. This kid never ceased to amaze me. A doctor indeed! So far no girl had moved outside of this tribe; even for those who had graduated from high school, it was simply not considered an option. Could she be the first? She certainly had great potential and I would love to be able to support her. I'd have to, since her parents had nothing, even if I could get them to agree to it. But the odds against that happening were huge.

I knew that deep down the only lasting thing I could give Eugenia would be an education. But that would mean becoming westernized. The few Nigerian doctors I had met were all trained in the UK, and I could well imagine the impact on her and her family. She would certainly develop a different view of tribal authority, and with that, the authority of her parents. The sense of independence that I was already noting in her would be enhanced; she certainly would not agree to an arranged marriage, and once she became accustomed to a different quality of life, would probably come home only for short visits. She would rapidly develop social and material needs that far surpassed what her native village could offer.

It was ironic that as much as I wanted local people to progress and grow prosperous, I could not disentangle this good intention from the questionable legacy of British colonialism. Nigeria was, after all, essentially an invention of the British Empire, creating a single Western-style republic out of a populous and culturally diverse region of West Africa in 1914. A truly Nigerian culture still exists at the tribal level, but it has never achieved what we would think of as a national identity. In a country with over five hundred languages, unity was approximated by teaching people to speak English. Schools, colleges, radio stations, magazines, and newspapers thus all came to be based on a Western model.

For Eugenia, this would mean that there was no way to "progress" and remain essentially Nigerian. In some ways I wanted her to remain a little Igedde girl just the way she was, but this was impossible. Her identity would change over time almost in spite of herself, even if she remained in her tribe.

In fact, Eugenia could see a symbol of her culture's surrender to the West each day she walked to school. Years ago the Igedde people had been famous for making their own iron implements, chiefly hoes and knives. There were local deposits of raw iron ore and they knew how to smelt it. But with the importation of cheaper Western implements, there was no need for native smelting, and no one in the tribe now remembered how to do it. The tall clay kilns that had smelted the iron and produced Igedde tools for decades, had been abandoned fifty years ago, but still remained standing.

"We must go now," Eugenia said abruptly, as if she'd had enough of my distracted reverie. "My mother will need help in preparing the evening meal. I will come back tomorrow so you can give me another book to read. Thank you for the drink, Barrington. Shall we take the cups back into your house?"

"No, there is no need," I replied, gathering them up. "I can manage."

With that the girls picked up their bags and walked off, hand in hand, along a narrow bush path towards the hills. I stood watching them until they looked back once to wave, and I waved back just before the tall elephant grass that lined both sides of the narrow path hid them from view. And then my worries about Eugenia became more personal.

Outside my own family I'd never spent any time with a young and gifted girl. My seminary training virtually ignored the existence of women; we were an enclosed society, created by men, for men, and controlled by men. In my seven years of training I never once heard a lecture or experienced a class discussion about sexual issues. It was a taboo subject, strictly off limits. Marriage, for instance, was simply a theoretical topic of theology and pastoral ministry. We had no personal interest since it was not an option in our lives.

Prior to the seminary, I had spent all my middle school and high school years in a male boarding school system where no women were allowed. Now twenty-nine years old, I had never experienced any kind of emotional involvement with a woman outside my own family. I had no idea what it was like to fall in or out of love, or experience the joys and the angst of the special relationships that my sisters had told me about.

So I was bothered by more than Eugenia's cultural identity. I was living on my own and in spite of a heavy work load in a very busy parish, I was lonely. I enjoyed her company that much I could admit. She reminded me of myself as a child: always asking questions, articulate, a voracious reader, acting very adult. But Eugenia was stirring so many things in me at once that I couldn't sort them all out.

While I was relaxing on the patio one evening a couple of weeks later, I suddenly realized that she hadn't visited me for a while. I called Alfred, my houseboy, and asked if he had seen her; he came from the hamlet next to hers. It was located on a very steep hillside about a half mile away, directly opposite our compound, but as the crow flies was much closer and would have been quite visible from the mission house except for the density of the jungle. Okigwe, Eugenia's father, was the headman there and we were good friends.

"Didn't you know that she is in her father's compound?" he asked in amazement. "Everybody knows that she is very sick."

"No," I responded with concern. I was irritated that my catechist, Christopher Okwoche, whom I paid to be my eyes and ears in the villages, had not reported anything to me. "Please go and find Okwoche and ask him to come here immediately."

Since it was late afternoon on the day of the open-air market where people from the surrounding area brought in their produce and goods for sale, including native beer and palm wine, I suspected where Okwoche might be. He spent most market days meeting Christians from remote outstations, people who often brought him a calabash of palm wine, his favorite tipple. I soon saw Okwoche, however, wobbling his way up our long driveway on his old bicycle, his white *riga* billowing out in the breeze and the unmistakable red fez-like hat stuck on his head. Once he got close, there was no questioning where he had been. Oozing perspiration, the smell of palm wine on him was almost overpowering. Dispensing with our usual greetings, I asked, "Okwoche, why did you not tell me about Eugenia? I hear that she is quite sick."

Looking distinctly uncomfortable, he avoided confrontation in true Nigerian fashion. "I will take the Father to her compound immediately,"

Eugenia looked very fragile lying on her native bamboo bed, little more than a pallet, with a multi-colored sheet covering her body. Her mother squatted at her side, gently wafting away the constant swarms of flies with a palm frond. It was stifling hot in the small room, with not a wisp of a breeze. Heavy beads of sweat on Eugenia's forehead created small rivulets that trickled down the side of her face and neck. Her shoulders and the top of her breasts were covered with a smelly black paste.

"She has been very ill for more than a week," her mother said to Okwoche, who translated for me. "Nobody here can explain what it is. Her father has insisted that she be treated by the village medicine man."

"What the heck are they doing with her?" I whispered to Okwoche.

"The people of this hamlet have a very strong medicine man," he explained. "You know who I am talking about. He is very powerful and the family will not go against anything he says. You know that this is one way he makes a lot of money." He pointed to a corner of the house where there was heap of what looked like burned rubbish and feathers stuffed into a red clay pot. "Look, he has sacrificed several hens and created an expensive 'Ju-Ju' to drive away Eugenia's sickness."

I knew that some real and effective medicine men did exist; I had once met a native bone setter and watched him work brilliantly on a broken leg. At the seminary in Keffi, the boys' cook always treated students who had malarial fever with amazing success. He was a true herbalist. But this "Ju-Ju" man was a charlatan. I had met him on a couple of occasions, and it was clear that he feared me. Each time I saw him, he tried to hide, and once when I walked close to his house, he dropped a load of firewood he was carrying and ran off into a field of tall corn plants.

Though Eugenia clearly had a fever, she smiled at me. Speaking slowly, she said, "So you have come to my home again, Barrington. I am sorry that I cannot prepare food for you. When I am better I will kill a chicken for you." Her once mischievous and lustrous eyes, were now bloodshot and a dirty shade of yellow. Her normally glowing face looked pale, and even through the perspiration, her skin lacked luster.

Crouching at the side of her cot, I ignored the discomfort of my bare knees pressing against the hard mud floor. All I wanted to do was to take care of this wonderful little girl, to make her well again. We were able to chat a little, and I anointed her with holy oil and gave her the sacrament of the sick. The tiny mud hut had slowly filled with villagers, waiting with curious expectation to see what I would do. When I was finished, I leaned over and gave her a final blessing. As I was about to leave, she turned her head toward me. "Remember, Barrington, if you become sick, I will come and help take care of you."

"Then you must first get well yourself and become strong," I replied, forcing myself to smile.

After that brief exchange I blessed everyone in the house and went outside, thankful for the fresh air but very disturbed at Eugenia's condition. The crowd followed me out, and Eugenia's mother begged me to stay so she could cook for me. But food was the last thing on my mind. The nearest hospital was fifty miles away across the bush; I suggested that I take Eugenia there, but her parents were adamant. Her father insisted that the local medicine man would make her well. I drew Okwoche to one side and quietly asked, "Christopher, did the medicine man make the black sludge on Eugenia's body?"

"Yes," he said. "The medicine man is in control here. But that stuff will not do anything for her. I think that she has yellow fever."

"Is there something else I should do?"

"No, Father," he said. "She is very, very sick, but the parents will not release her. In any case," he continued, "we cannot take her to the hospital in Otrukpo since they are only admitting military wounded. She is better off here."

"You're probably right," I replied, although I was reluctant to leave Eugenia to her current circumstances. *Should I take her to the hospital anyway and try to get the military to admit her? Then I realized that the journey over the almost impassible bush roads would probably weaken her further. And if the military turned us away, which was their normal practice, then we would have to repeat the painful journey back.*

Two days later, in the evening while I was coaching the school soccer team, I heard blood-chilling cries coming from the hamlet up on the hillside. Intuitively I knew what had happened. I didn't even bother to change from my sweaty dirty clothes. I ran as fast as I could, scrambling, slipping and sliding on the narrow path as it wound its way up the steep hillside to Okigwe's compound. Outside Eugenia's hut, the women had bared their breasts and were throwing white ashes over themselves. They were screaming in a chilling and eerie way that made the hair on the back of my neck stand up.

Okigwe, Eugenia's father, was sitting on a tiny stool under a makeshift awning of woven palm fronds at the side of the house, surrounded by his kindred and elders from neighboring compounds. I squatted next to him as we exchanged the traditional greetings and I offered my condolences. His oldest son Akuso helped translate for us. Holding on to my hand, the old man surprised me by saying, "She is yours now, Barrington. You can have her. She told us you were her Father."

I was taken aback, unsure of what he meant. "What would you like me to do, Okigwe?"

He seemed to frown at first as if he did not understand my question, so I repeated it. As he replied, the look on his face was clearly that of a father explaining to his ignorant son what his obligations were. "She is yours, Barrington. She belongs to you. You must take her to your compound."

I was surprised, but also flooded with guilt. If Okigwe was this willing to let me bury Eugenia, then perhaps I should have applied more pressure earlier and insisted on taking her to the mission compound, away from the medicine man. At least she would have rested better, and there I had some means to help control her temperature. Why hadn't I been more assertive? How could he be handing over his dead daughter to me? By all rights she should be alive, teasing me, asking me for another book, her bubbly personality making people happy with her laughter.

"Of course," I answered, finally comprehending. "I will take her early in the morning," I said gently, "and we will bury her next to the church, if that will please you."

"Do it," he said with great sadness in his eyes. "She will rest well there. She is yours."

I was choking with emotion, struggling to hold back my tears. My sense of loss was almost overpowering. What was happening to me? Why did I feel this way? It was not rational, but somehow I knew that I needed to listen carefully to the voice within me crying to be heard. Through the jumbled, turbulent cacophony in my head, came a gentle whisper that riveted me, piercing me to the core as it repeated: *She was your daughter, she was your daughter.*

I made the trek down the steep and narrow hillside path, lost in my own thoughts, speaking to no one. But once in the quiet of my own room, I cried a lot that night. A person that young, so vivacious and with so much potential, should not die. I was angry that there was no modern medicine available for Eugenia and frustrated that her parents had turned to the local medicine man. Why hadn't Okwoche or Alfred told me earlier about Eugenia's illness? The fatalism of the Igedde people regarding sickness and death, their lack of urgency borne out of being dirt poor with almost no resources, made me both sad and angry. I was also frustrated at my helplessness.

It was my first funeral in Igedde, and in fact the first child's funeral service I had ever performed. I had never even seen a dead child before, let alone one with whom I had talked and played and shared her dreams.

We buried her in the soft light and coolness of the early morning. I had spent time with Okwoche planning the actual ceremony, making it as relevant as I could. We brought in native drummers, the school kids sang, and the women danced in a slow, rhythmic fashion as we processed to the hastily dug grave, just a short distance from the church. As the first shovel of dirt landed on the simple white wooden coffin, the women simultaneously began to wail. It was a spine-chilling, primordial sound of unrestricted despair.

Afterward I walked for hours up and down the tree-lined driveway between the mission house and the church alongside which Eugenia was now buried, trying to pray. But it was in vain. I could not stop my mind from bringing back vivid memories of her bright smile, cheery voice, and the precious moments we had together. I paused occasionally in my stride to try to recapture some of the details, as if standing still would bring them all back. I lost all track of time.

I had realized from the outset that our relationship had been very special, but it was Eugenia who had seen right through me and made me understand what it was really all about. Everything in my seminary training dictated against it, but now I had to admit that I really loved this little girl as a daughter. I'd wanted to be a real father to her, to take care of her, to nurture her and provide for her well-being. I wanted the best of everything for her. But in her time of greatest crisis, the little girl who wanted to become a doctor didn't really need a priest; she needed a skilled Western physician. And now she was gone.

Before my time in Nigeria was over, I would minister at many more funerals of children, and each time it would reopen the wound. After all these years the memories and emotions come flooding back at full force, even as I write. I still feel guilty that somehow I did not do enough, that somehow I could have saved Eugenia.

CHAPTER 5

Sickness & Caring

The letter was brief and to the point: "Your new pastor has arrived and is waiting for you at Mt. St. Michael's College, Aliade. Please arrange to pick him up as soon as possible." After almost five months of being on my own, I would finally have a co-worker.

He was just as I remembered him, a small, rotund red-faced Yorkshire man in his early fifties, very neatly dressed in starched, white shirt and khaki shorts, the inevitable cigarette gripped between his nicotine-stained fingers, white, knee-length socks covering his equally white spindly legs. We had met just very briefly about six months previously when both of us were collecting mail and supplies from the Bishop's House in Makurdi. He had only heard very vaguely about me, and that I had originally been as- signed to teach in the seminary in Keffi prior to my assignment in Igedde. There was something very appealing about this man. Wally Duffy's quiet gentleness and warm kindness seemed very genuine.

As just the two of us were having a very early breakfast, I informed him that as soon as we got back to the mission, I would be setting out on a long safari, visiting many villages in the Igedde hills. I really wanted to do this, but if truth were told, it had all been prompted by a silly discussion the previous evening when a group of older priests were making fun of and criticizing the younger priests, me included. I was pointedly told to "keep my mouth shut and my bowels open" and "get my knees brown" before anybody would pay attention to what I might have to say. It was really a case of the "old" school versus the "new." In my own mind I was determined that I would show them and everybody else that I was up to the task, and would make my mark as a missionary.

Since these old "sweats" put a great deal of importance to going on safari, spending time trekking to villages and spreading the gospel message, I would prove that I was really serious about my work by going out on safari for at least two weeks, when most people only went out for one. I would then return just to get some supplies and wouldn't even spend the night in the mission. Instead, I'd take off again for another week or two. Wally, of course, had no idea what I really had in mind.

"But is this the time to do that, Mike?" he questioned. "It's still raining almost every day, and I'm sure the bush roads will be almost impassible. And won't it be very difficult, if not dangerous, trekking up in the hills?"

He was absolutely right of course, but I was already stubbornly formulating my plan.

"It's been almost twenty years since I was in this area and you will certainly have to give me a crash course in how the mission has developed and grown, but I'm sure the hills haven't changed much," Wally added with a chuckle. Then becoming serious again, he added, "Think about it, Mike: it's not always safe trekking anywhere in this area during the rainy season. Just take it from an old timer like me. In my younger days I also wanted to do, and sometimes did, those types of crazy things, but I'm a little smarter now. I knew that my decisions then were not the best, even if my intentions were. Yes, it's God's work and it's for the poor people. But if you get sick or hurt so you cannot work, you will be no good to either of them."

His appeal fell on deaf ears. I had my made my mind up.

"Well, if you must go, then plan it carefully," he mumbled, lighting yet another cigarette. I was just discovering that he really was a chain smoker.

"You know Igedde much better than me, so I will trust your judgment, Mike," was all he said, and that was that.

Things did not quite go as planned.

It was a Friday mid-afternoon and the big market day for our area. As we drove through it, I recognized many of our parishioners who waved and called out to us as we passed. It felt good to be home and although I had only been in Igedde a relatively short time, I was already beginning to feel that that this is where I belonged.

An hour after our return, our catechist Okwoche came pedaling up the driveway and shouting at the top of his lungs, "Father Mike, Father Mike come quickly."

"What is it, Okwoche?" I asked, walking out on to the verandah to meet him.

"There has been a terrible accident near Ikache clinic. A mammy-wagon has fallen from the bridge. Many people are wounded."

Without saying a word I rushed into the office and grabbed my first aid kit and the holy oil used for anointing the sick. Wally had come out of his room to see what the shouting was all about. I quickly told him, "There's been a bad motor accident, so I'll go and see what I can do."

It was far worse than I expected. Most of the wooden bridges in the area had either been blown up or damaged by the military. This one had been damaged. Most of the top deck was missing and vehicles tried to cross by bringing their own planks. Trucks crossed over by laying the planks in front of the wheels, and when the vehicle had passed over them, picking them up from behind and starting the process all over again. It was a slow and very dangerous but effective method.

In this particular case the driver had moved too close to the edge of one of the planks; it had flipped over and the wagon had fallen into a shallow stream thirty feet below. The wagon had left the market fully loaded with sacks of rice and many passengers were perched on top. In the fall, the passengers had tumbled into the stream first, and then the sacks, and finally the wagon had come crashing down onto them.

The wagon had been heading for Ogoja, a neighboring state that was deeper into the war zone, and it appeared that most of the passengers were from there. People were struggling frantically to pull the wounded out. Some were now sitting in a huddle, dazed, and nursing horrible head wounds; others clearly had broken limbs. It was also evident that several people had died since they were laid out on the bank and were completely covered by brightly colored cloth. All told, I counted about twenty-two injured people.

The clinic staff was doing its best to provide first aid, but they didn't have sufficient resources; the clinic itself was just a small, rural maternity center with no professional staff. I realized that some of the wounded were my teachers who were going home for the weekend and they were crying, begging me to carry them, and grasping my hands in desperation.

Things were so chaotic: I needed more time to evaluate the situation.

Okwoche worked with me as I anointed many of the sick. There was not much I could do. Their wounds were far beyond my limited "first aid" capability.

"Father," Okwoche pulled me to one side. "You are being asked if you will transport two dead bodies across the border into Ogoja. People are willing to pay a lot of money."

Since I had the only truck in the area, I was not surprised by the unusual request. However, I thought it best to try and help the more seriously wounded. There was no emergency care anywhere in Igedde, and Otrukpo Hospital, fifty miles away, was reserved for the military. There was no way I could help everybody. I had to make some quick but difficult decisions.

"Okwoche, I think it best to take some of the most seriously wounded across the border. These people are telling me that there is a small Christian clinic at Wannakum; do you know if it is so?"

"Yes, Father, but it also is now in the hands of the military. It will soon be night and there are many broken bridges that must be crossed. There is also a military checkpoint to be passed, and because it is in the active war zone there is a strict curfew in place."

"We must move quickly then," I urged. "Help me select the people to travel with us."

Our total count was ten people; that was all I felt I could safely carry. I also needed an extra pair of strong hands to help in placing our planks on the broken bridges so I quickly drove back to the mission to let Wally know what the situation was. He was walking up and down on the verandah reading his prayer book as I arrived, and his concern was evident when I told him my intentions.

"It's dangerous crossing the border, Mike, even during the day. At night anything can happen and especially so since there is a curfew. And God help you in crossing the bridges. Do take care, lad. I'll be praying for you. Let me get a bottle of cold water for you: you'll probably need it later on."

Alfred, my houseboy, had come out to see if he was needed, so I had him fill the truck with gas and fasten two extra jerry cans on the front bumper, collect our flashlights, and throw the planks we always carried in the rainy season into the back of the truck. Since he was strong and reliable, I asked him to come along and this gave Wally some comfort.

"I'm glad you are taking him, Mike, he will be a big help."

Carrying a group of seriously wounded, moaning and crying people on a bone-jarring journey for several hours in the dark, was stressful to say the least. We crossed so many broken bridges I lost count. I needed to get out to inspect each one before I attempted to cross, and each time Alfred and Okwoche worked by flashlight with the planks and guided me over. It was slow, dangerous, tiring and nerve-wracking work.

The one major surprise of the night was at the military checkpoint. Once the soldiers came close with their bush lamps and saw all the wounded, it was clear to them what I was doing. After the usual posturing, they understood and I was allowed to pass as far as the clinic where I intended simply to leave everybody. They also said they would clear me to pass on my return.

The clinic was in almost complete darkness when we arrived, except for two armed soldiers on guard duty in a makeshift gate house lit with a small kerosene lamp. After a brief explanation, and an examination of the passengers, one of them strode off into the darkness and after a short while returned with two nurses. They introduced themselves; one a local girl and the other an American midwife, Elanor, who was in charge. She told me that she had been at the clinic for nine years. There was no electricity but in the glow of her bush light I could see the strain and anxiety in her face. She explained that this used to be a maternity clinic but now was full of wounded soldiers. Since there was no more bed space and almost no medications she begged me not to leave our wounded passengers there. While I was explaining to her that the wounded were from this region and I could not take them back with me, they had gotten out of the truck and were seated or lying on the ground. She was quite distraught at seeing so many people, and repeated in a quivering voice that they had no means of treating these patients. It was only then that I could see that she was actually in tears.

"If that is the case, then they will all have to take care of themselves and make their own way home," I said. "I am so sorry to have brought you this problem, but I too am taking a big risk and am breaking the curfew. It is really dangerous for me to be here."

We shook hands and I wished her well, my thoughts already focusing on the hazardous and long journey home.

Alfred had filled up the truck with gas and was replacing a jerry can in its rack, and I was about to start the motor when Elanor came over. "Mike," she asked, "I hate to ask, but do you have any gas left that you could sell to me?"

"What do you mean?" I said.

"I have not been able to drive our truck for six weeks, and I am really afraid that if the fighting moves this way again, I will not be able to get out. The military have commandeered all the gas and took our reserves. No gas stations have functioned in this area since the war started. We have to cross the border to get it and even then we could get stopped. A local officer siphoned out my gas tank weeks ago and so I am stuck, I was just praying that somebody would come and help me out."

"Yes, of course," I said. In fact we have an empty plastic container in the back, I'll ask Alfred to fill it for you. It will give you about five gallons, enough to get you out of the war zone or at least away from immediate danger, if you can keep it safely hidden. And forget any payment, one day I might really need your help."

It was almost daybreak when I got back to Igedde. The sun had not quite made it up over the Igedde hills, but as I crossed the final bridge I could see and hear people down below, still working through the crash site with the aid of flash lights. There was nothing more I could do; there was no need talk to anybody. The dead would be taken away and buried later on in the day. The wounded would just have to manage as best they could.

Back at the mission, Joseph, our cook, had made coffee for all three of us. As we sat there in the sitting room looking dirty, disheveled, and exhausted, we did not say much; there was nothing much to say other than to admit that we had done the right thing. We had helped a few people.

Through the open double doors I was witnessing a blood red sun beginning to peek over the beautiful Igedde hills, and as if caught on the high peaks, slowly bleed down into the valley covering it with a golden mantle. It was the beginning of another precious African morning and the start of a new day. It just felt good to be here.

It took me about six days to put my safari together, checking all my gear, making sure that I had everything I needed, and most importantly hearing from Okwoche that all the villages where we would be staying had been notified. This would be a very challenging trek, and once into the hills, it would be difficult to double back if anything was missing.

Wally hovered over me like a mother hen, checking the amount of food I was taking, especially filtered water, and ensuring I had sufficient toilet paper. He stood on the verandah watching everything as I started to leave.

"Take care, lad, and don't do anything stupid," he gently chided. "You might have difficulty getting good reception from the BBC behind the hills, so I'll be sure to keep the soccer scores for you, but do keep tuning in just in case you can get a signal. You need to keep tabs on the military movements and the state of the war. Remember, the Bishop insists that we listen to the local news at least a couple of times a day."

He was so genuinely thoughtful.

"Don't worry about me," I said, climbing into my truck. "And please make sure the new boy, Oliver, feeds my parrot."

As I eased my truck into gear, my two German shepherd dogs ran alongside barking until I reached the end of the driveway. Wally continued waving from the verandah until the trees blocked him from view. I was saddened that this caring man, after all his years of experience, would be reduced to saying a morning Mass in the parish church, and one Mass on Sunday, then simply spending the rest of each day as best he could, which I later discovered was mainly just reading novels.

In the short time we had been together, Wally had demonstrated how he wanted to live his missionary life. He generally stayed housebound, occasionally meeting somebody from the parish who came needing assistance, but more often than not, making sure the house sparkled, the floors were polished every day, and water was pumped from the well for the toilets and showers. He would listen to the radio, the BBC World Service special broadcast to West Africa every night at seven o'clock, a ritual I was learning that must never be interrupted.

Ministering to people who had not seen a priest in months and in some cases a year, was extremely satisfying for me, and I never ceased to be amazed how people clung to their faith with very little support. They were extremely poor and burdened by the harshness of their lives, since they lived high up in the hills in small scattered hamlets and villages, eking out an existence by farming the steep stony slopes. But as I arrived in each place, their welcome was always warm and genuine.

Twelve days later, dirty and worn out, I returned to the mission. Taking a regular shower felt wonderful, and changing into some really dry clean clothes had never felt so good. Wally and I had lunch together. I was eager to hear about the state of the war since my radio had only functioned inconsistently, and sometimes I was just too tired to tune in.

We briefly brought each other up to date, and then towards the end of the meal, in his own gentle way, he asked me, "Mike, do you think you're doing the right thing by going out again? The rains are terrible, and it must be very difficult out there in the bush."

I was not to be deterred.

"It's not too bad," I bluffed, "and in any case, there is so much work to be done. So many villages have not seen a priest for ages."

"Do take care and make sure that you eat well," he added. "Your health is very important."

With all of my supplies replenished, and Wally's reluctant blessing, I headed off into a very difficult region, criss-crossed by streams and small rivers where the roads were always bad, and at this time of the year almost impassable. All in all, I stayed out another nine days, and the last three or four were completely miserable, in spite of the fact that I was spiritually very happy.

The rains were incessant and at times the clouds touching the tops of the tall jungle cast an air of grayness and gloom over everything. The actual trekking, once we had left the truck in a tiny village, became so difficult that I decided to take my boots off and walk barefoot. We were constantly up to our knees in either mud or flowing water. In one place a small bridge had been washed away, and the villagers had replaced it with a narrow tree trunk about fourteen feet long. Alfred and Okwoche had no problem negotiating what to me was an obstacle, even with heavy loads on their heads. Just by looking at it, I knew I wouldn't be able to cross; the log was only about fifteen inches wide and the rain was coming down in buckets.

"Can you come back and help me?" I shouted over to Alfred.

"Is the Father afraid to cross?" he laughed back at me.

"Yes, I am," I replied unashamedly.

In seconds he dropped his load under a bush, bounded over without so much as a look at the water raging below, and stood beside me. I was so envious of his agility.

"Here," he said tapping his left shoulder with a sopping wet hand. "Hold me here and I will lead you."

The first steps seemed easy as I carefully planted my feet on the log. It had been stripped of its bark and together with the rain presented what was for me a slippery and insecure platform. I tried sliding my feet, one behind the other, instead of taking normal steps. At first this seemed to work until I was about three-quarters of the way across. My mistake was looking down at my feet and being momentarily distracted by the fast-flowing, dirty brown water five feet below me.

Hitting the water didn't surprise me as much as feeling myself being dragged under by the weight of my rucksack. I am a fairly strong swimmer and it was not too difficult to juggle free from the straps and release the pack. It eventually floated downstream to the bank where Okwoche, reaching out with a fallen tree branch, managed to recover it. Alfred ran down the bank and helped haul me out about thirty yards further down. Both of them could not stop laughing.

My immediate concern was for my rucksack. It was supposed to be waterproof and it contained all of my spare clothing. Other than being soaked, I was actually fine. We all huddled together under the relatively dry shade of a giant cotton tree, where an initial inspection revealed that most of my clothes in the rucksack were wet. It was decision time. Should I return to the mission and pick up fresh clothes and disappoint the people who were waiting for me in the villages ahead or should I continue as planned? It was an easy decision: at that moment my ministry was the most important thing in my life.

The rest of that week was a miserable experience. Everywhere we went the mosquitoes were a serious problem. Sitting together each evening, we often ate indecipherable but tasty, native food by firelight, the smoke filling the small windowless mud hut and making our eyes water. We were hoping that by not using our kerosene bush lamps fewer mosquitoes would be attracted, but it didn't seem to make much difference. I continued to be eaten alive, and it was a relief to finally get under my net.

Changing from one set of wet and damp clothes for some just less so and a lack of sufficient sleep began to take their toll. I was developing a hacking cough and I became irritable. Physically I was quite tired. The wound on the heel of my left foot caused by not wearing boots had now become worse. It was inflamed and infected and was not responding to my first aid. I simply could not keep the wound clean and dry.

I asked a villager with a bicycle to travel across the bush and let Wally know that I would be returning. He could reach the mission in two days. It would take me at least three or four to get home. But I knew I needed to take care of myself better than I was doing, and I needed some warm dry clothing.

As I turned my truck onto the mission driveway, it just felt good to be back. I was very tired and hungry, with the makings of a full beard, and my clothes were covered with red mud since we'd had to dig the truck out twice. But my spirits were strong, and I felt very humbled and grateful that I had been chosen to do this special kind of priestly work.

"Eh, lad, you look like you've had a rough time. Welcome," was Wally's opening greeting. "I got your message and thank you for that."

He was standing on the verandah wearing his freshly pressed clothes. The inevitable cigarette hung between the fingers of one hand, the other was held out towards me. He was always so particular about his dress, and in contrast to myself and where I had just come from, he seemed a little out of place rather like a Marlboro advertisement in some glossy magazine.

"There's lots of water for a shower, Mike, and I've told the cook to prepare a big meal. I'm sure you're fed up with bush chicken, so I got some beef from the market. Whenever you're ready, come and sit down, and we can enjoy a beer together."

Just changing into dry, warm and clean clothes, made me feel like a different person. The rain had started up again, a real tropical downpour with incessant flashes of lightning and thunder. That, plus the noise of the rain on the metal roof made conversation difficult, so we drew our chairs closer together.

"Well, lad, it's good to have you back. So how was it?" he asked, leaning across so I could hear him better.

"It's difficult to know where to begin," I responded, "but I'll do my best."

I briefly gave him some of the high points of the safari, reading sections from my logbook, now so mildewed the covers were beginning to come loose. In places the ink had started to run a little and the pages were wrinkled and damp. I told him about the numbers of people I had baptized, of a very remote village called Ugbada where there was a need to help more with the school, and where the elders had requested assistance with building a clinic. I also shared my story of falling into the stream. He seemed impressed with what I had achieved, especially with the number of villages I had reached, and he let me go on until I felt that there was little else left to say. Then, he half-turned towards me, looking at his hand as he carefully placed his beer glass on the small table next to his chair, and hesitantly asked, "Look, lad, don't you like me?"

Although surprised by the question, I could answer it honestly. "Of course I like you, Wally, so why the question?"

"Well, in all my years, I've never been with anybody who wanted to stay out so long on safari. It's almost as if you didn't like my company. I've missed you, you know. It can get very lonely with only the cook and a couple of houseboys around, and they hardly speak English."

"I missed you, too, and as much as I love my work, it's nice to have a place to come back to. And in any case with these rains continuing, I don't think I will be going out for a while."

It all seemed so far away, that crazy meeting in Aliade almost a month ago. It seemed so different now, but how was I to share what was really going on inside of me? How could I expect Wally to understand, even if I could articulate it? He was clearly of a different generation, and in any case I really knew very little about him. We had shared very little of our personal lives.

"I saw something rather interesting while on the other side of the hills," I said, suddenly remembering the incident. He was on his feet walking towards the refrigerator.

"Are you ready for another, Mike? I put plenty in knowing that you were on your way back."

As if that would have made any difference. Don't use me as an excuse for your boozing. You know why you keep it full of beer. And right now I'm not in the mood to placate you.

"No thanks, Wally," I replied, holding up my glass so he could see I had quite an amount remaining. "I'm still working on this one."

He flopped down into his favorite chair, pouring the liquid with the attention of a chemist, then set the bottle down on the side table. Reaching out his left hand, he picked up his cigarettes and lighter, and with a motion and expertise borne out of years of practice, he extricated one, lit it almost like a one-armed robot, and inhaled deeply.

"You started to tell me something, Mike; what was it? Please continue."

"You have heard me talk about the Migili tribe, and how normally they are completely nude except for a bunch of twigs with leaves covering their lower body, back and front. Well, apparently a small group of them regularly cross over the border from Ogoja to a bush market near one of our outstations. I got to visit with them a little; they are extremely shy and speak only a few words of Igedde. What surprised me the most was that they were all wearing a sort of purple skirt, both men and women, but they still all had the bunches of leaves on top."

"You mean that somebody is trying to make them wear clothes?" Wally asked in amazement.

"Absolutely," I replied. I knew that there was a Protestant mission over there that was dedicated to working with these people; I have seen some of the bible translations they have done. Well, it appears that the pastors, a Dutch couple, are offended by Migili nudity. I guess they brought in a few thousand yards of this purple material and they give it out for free. I'm told that they will not allow people into their church unless they are covered."

"Holy shit," he said. "They must be crazy if they believe they can change a culture by doing that."

"I agree totally. They will change nothing. People will adapt so that they can benefit from the best of both worlds. I just find it very sad. But hey, look at the Catholic Church out here. For the past hundred and fifty years we have been mumbling away in Latin, expecting people to come to mass and participate, even though they did not understand a word, as if that was just fine. But don't get me going on this. You already know where I stand."

"You're right, lad," he replied knowingly," why don't we just eat and we can talk some more in the morning?"

The rain intensified, hammering so hard on the roof that it made any further conversation almost impossible. After my first decent meal in weeks I went directly to bed. I was exhausted.

I was awakened by the constant thump, thump, thump of a mortar and pestle. I instinctively knew the cook was preparing yams. I also realized that the same noise was in my head. I had a beast of a headache and was not feeling very well at all. Even taking a shower and getting dressed seemed to demand a superhuman effort. I had no energy.

"You don't look so good, lad," announced Wally quizzically, scrutinizing my face.

He was in the family room, sitting in his favorite chair, smoking and reading an old paperback. It was midmorning and what else would he be doing? If people didn't come to him, then in his mind he had no work to do. The office was closed.

"I thought you'd be tired so I did not want to disturb you. Should I ask the cook to fix you something, or will you wait for lunch?"

"No thanks, Wally," I replied, "I am not too hungry. A cup of coffee would be great, though. Please have Joseph bring it to the office; I'm going to go and work on completing my safari journal."

There was so much more I had to record before it slipped my memory. I also wanted to re-read the incident reports that I had briefly noted. Thankfully, the rains had stopped, though it was still heavily overcast. Sitting at my desk in front of the open louver windows, I watched our ducks and hens enjoying the large pools of water in front of the house. The trees dripped off the last of the rain and the ground steamed under the watery, mid-morning sun like some sort of giant sauna. I was reflecting on where I had been up in the Igedde hills, and normally the hills presented a beautiful backdrop to the mission house. But this morning the cloud cover was so low I couldn't even make out the tree tops of the jungle two hundred yards away.

By mid-day I realized I had a temperature, complete with a thumping headache and now diarrhea. I tried to lie down. But that only made me feel worse; the room seemed to be swaying from side to side. If I closed my eyes, I began to feel even more dizzy and nauseous. I was a little concerned about having "the runs" since I had forgotten to get a supply of preventative medication when I went to collect Wally in Aliade.

He was still sitting in the same place when I entered the sitting room, except now he had a bottle of beer on his side-table and a glass in his hand.

"Wally, I'm literally feeling like shit," I said, "and I have nothing to take for this diarrhea. Have you anything in your room?"

"Eh, I'm sorry, lad. No, I can't help you. I guess you must have eaten something in the bush that didn't agree with you. Why don't you run over to Ikache, and see if they can give you something?"

"Yes, that's a smart idea," I agreed, already moving to get my keys. "I should have thought about that earlier."

I had to pause for a moment as I stretched out my hand to reach for my keys, holding on to my desk as the room started slowly spinning. *"What the heck is happening to me?" I asked myself. "I have never ever felt like this before."*

Ikache was a hamlet with a small, rudimentary maternity clinic just a few miles away. It had no water or electricity and no doctor, but I had heard that there was a visiting expatriate midwife there with her husband who was a preacher. Both belonged to a Protestant group from Germany. But driving myself there was a mistake.

I was informed that the European staff were away, leaving only a local aide in charge. I asked if I could use the toilet, and instead of directing me to the staff bathroom, I was sent to a "native" affair, behind the main building, a small mud house with a hole in the ground. My head was thumping so much I never for a second thought of insisting on using the staff facilities.

In a daze, I crouched down to enter through the tiny doorway, but the heat inside, the disgusting condition of the floor, the smells, and the flies were too much for me to handle. In addition to my diarrhea, I now started to throw up. There was no toilet paper, and I can vaguely remember trying to tear off a section of my shirt so I could clean myself. I somehow got back to the mission, hit my bathroom again, and this time collapsed on my bed.

The next three days were a blur. I don't know how I managed to be in bed wearing a T-shirt, something I never did, and was smothered in blankets. I remember seeing Wally standing at the foot of my bed saying,

"I know you don't like me, lad, and I know it will hurt you, but I need to move you."

All three houseboys were there, as well as the cook and the catechist talking in hushed tones, their somber faces looking as if they were at a funeral. Wally made them get a fresh dry blanket to wrap me in, and I felt two of them carry me to an armchair in the corner of my room. Meanwhile, the others stripped my bed, removed the mattress, turned it over and re-made it, and gently lifted me back onto it. They removed all my clothes, and holding me like a rag doll, gently put clean dry ones on me. I was having my first bout of malarial fever and it was a bad one.

Wally was wonderful. He placed a bucket at the side of my bed and told me, "You probably won't make it across to your bathroom so use this. You don't have to worry about the boys seeing anything; I'll take care of it myself."

For three days, I floated in and out of a delirium. I was totally helpless. I have no idea how much time Wally spent watching and praying over me, sponging me down, placing an ice pack on my head, and dosing me three times a day with anti-malarial medication, which we had lots of, thank God, and force-feeding me liquids.

By the fourth day, I was coming out of the fever, and my temperature was beginning to drop. By the fifth day, it was almost normal. However, I hadn't eaten for several days and that plus the diarrhea and my loss of fluid through sweating had made my legs so weak they wouldn't hold me. I still couldn't make it to the bathroom. When I finally got up, it was another three or four days before I could walk around the house without fear of falling. Wally told me very little other than that it had been a serious fever, and I had always been told that your first bout of malaria is always the worst.

We had run out of mattresses! My perspiration had gone right through my mattress and formed a puddle under the bed. Wally had first taken the mattress from the visitor's room. Because it was difficult to get them dried out, — it was after all the height of the rainy season, — he had finally taken the one from his own bed. Each time my perspiration went right through the mattress.

I asked Wally, "What happened to me?"

"You've had a bad one, son," he mumbled, "but you're on the mend now. Malarial fever; it's a bastard, but you're over the worst of it now."

"But I can't remember much about it," I insisted.

"You don't need to, Mike," he chided, "you were delirious for long periods, cussed me out good and hollered at me like a madman, but that's all part of the fever. Never mind; now you need lots of rest and good food."

As soon as I felt well enough, I drove both of us to St. Michael's College in Aliade, the Spiritans' center, where I could recuperate for a while. My friend Jack, the principal of the college and a person I really respected, was a great host. In addition to his generosity, he was also very wise. He gave me a valuable piece of information that I was later able to pass on to others.

"The aftermath of a fever is worse than the damn fever itself, Mike. It's awful. It's just awful. I was depressed for months after my first fever. It took me a year to fully recover. I think the depression is in some ways worse than the fever itself."

How grateful I am that he said those words. Physically, I was almost back to my usual self within a couple of weeks, but for months I was weighed down with a terrible depression, frequent nightmares of falling into a big black hole, and constant, almost obsessive thoughts of death. And Jack was right; it probably took me close to a year before I truly felt myself again.

I blamed myself for getting sick, for my stupidity and pig-headedness, for being overtired and pushing myself too hard. I blamed myself for not listening to Wally. My tiredness probably was at the root of it all, which was probably why I forgot to take my daily anti-malaria medication.

I learned a couple of hard lessons through this sickness: that physical health is of primary importance and should never be taken for granted; the other was the value and need of a caring and sensitive companion.

It's strange as time passes, how sometimes a date will stick in one's mind, and for me September 17 is one of them. About six months after my sickness, just as Wally and I were strolling back from visiting the local elementary school, Sebastian Ubeke, our postman, came pedaling furiously up the driveway. Seeing us he waved, got down from his bicycle, and waited for us to arrive. Black patches of sweat were slowly spreading under the armpits of his light blue uniform jacket, and I noticed that the front of his pants was held together by a piece of white string since the regular button arrangement could not accommodate his bulging stomach. He removed his soft cloth cap, wiping his brow with it. I wondered whether his sweating was just the result of his exertions or because of his anxiety at having to meet us. Since he had taken a second wife several months ago and made her pregnant, he had stopped coming to Church.

"Good day, Reverend Fathers, I have a very important letter for you. It is from the State Government," he announced very formally. Then removing the leather satchel hanging from his shoulder, he painstakingly unfastened the buckles, reached inside and retrieved an envelope bearing the embossed coat of arms of Benue Plateau State. It was neither addressed to Wally or me, but simply to the "Pastor In Charge."

"Well, good day to you too, Ubeke," I replied. "I hope you are well. Thank you for coming to us."

"I thought it was my duty to make sure that this letter was placed directly in your hands," he said, bowing obsequiously and holding it with both hands and handing it over to Wally. "I think the Reverend Fathers can see that I am a conscientious civil servant. I can go now."

"Thank you," replied Wally nervously. And with that, Ubeke quickly turned his bicycle around, slowly re-mounted and headed off back to town.

"I hate receiving this kind of shit," he began as we continued our way towards the mission house. "You can only expect the worst. This damn government is certainly not going to give us anything."

I was not surprised when, as we sat down to have a beer before lunch, Wally handed me the letter. "Here, Mike, your eyes are sharper than mine; why don't you read it for both of us."

"I don't think you will like this, Wally," I announced, trying to mentally prepare him for what was coming next, but "all clergy and teachers are instructed to show up at the soccer stadium in Otrukpo; there are going to be public executions."

"You must be shitting me," he cried as if he could not believe his ears, reaching over the small side table that stood between us and grabbing my arm. "This is insanity. They can't ask us to do that." His fear-filled voice trembled with emotion.

"I'm sure it's no consolation to you Wally," I responded softly, giving his hand a reassuring pat, "but I too am certainly not looking forward to it. The fact is this is a command performance."

In one sense this was not a total surprise. The government needed to do something. Ever since the war ended six months ago, we had heard about ex-soldiers who were committing armed robbery, murders, and terrorizing communities. The Federal Government had failed to demobilize its troops in an orderly and accountable manner. As a result, many of the troops simply went back to their villages and families carrying weapons and ammunition. It was clear that the Government, realizing its mistake, was now trying to address the issue, to reassure the public, and wanted to make a clear public statement that such behavior would not be tolerated.

Otrukpo soccer stadium is not large. There were a few bleachers along one side of a regular-sized red-dirt playing field. The goal posts were still there, but an elevated dais had been constructed at the side of the center line, decorated with Nigerian flags and a big green and white banner that read, "One Nigeria." In front of one goal was a carefully arranged thick wall of sandbags, and in front of it were ten large posts about five feet apart, each one about eight feet high.

The place was crowded and as I looked around, I could see dotted here and there some of my colleagues standing with their teachers, and I wondered if they were feeling the same as me. I was distressed at seeing hundreds of young children from elementary schools occupying the front ranks, cheering and waving flags as if it was simply a day off from school, a kind of festival.

I hoped it would be quick, mainly because I did not want to be there, but also just because standing there under a blazing sun would soon become intolerable.

Right on time a stream of military and governmental dignitaries filed in as a military officer called their names over a PA system, each one taking his place on the dais. As military music began, a large detachment of armed soldiers in heavily starched uniforms entered, gave an impressive display of formation marching, and then in a very orderly fashion distributed itself in front of the crowd, standing to attention at regular fifteen foot intervals along the perimeter of the field.

The master of ceremonies asked everybody to stand for the arrival of the Governor. A shiny black Mercedes limousine drove slowly up to the dais steps, the State and Federal pennants on its front wings fluttering in the gentle breeze, and out stepped the Military Governor, resplendent in full dress uniform. Escorted by his own personal guards, he mounted the steps and stood to attention at center stage while the national anthem was played. The crowd cheered, waved their flags and cheered again. There were chants all around of "One Nigeria," repeated over and over.

His speech was brief, to the point, and left nobody in any doubt that armed crime would not be tolerated. There was no cheering. The speech was followed by a deafening, uncomfortable silence and all eyes focused on the field itself.

Suddenly I felt a hand come down hard on my shoulder.

"How's it going, Mike?" a familiar voice asked. Without turning around I knew who it was.

"And how are you doing, you old bastard?" I whispered, turning around and giving him a big hug. I hadn't seen Jim Brown, one of my close friends ever since college, for almost a year. "What brings you here? You're a long way from home."

Jim was pastor of Gboko parish about a hundred miles away in Tiv country. He looked tired and gaunt. His hair was also receding, but the smile and Scottish warmth in his voice was still the same.

"It's great to see you, Mike. I recognized you from over there," he said, waving his hand in the direction of the bleachers. "I was sitting with some military brass. One of these prisoners, is from my parish. I spent a couple of hours with him yesterday. They kept him in the local jail and moved him down here very early this morning He robbed a taxi at gunpoint and got almost nothing, the equivalent of a couple of dollars, but was caught by a mob of locals. I felt that I just had to come here and pray for him."

"Oh, my God! It must have been awful for you. I am so sorry."

"Well, I must admit, it's not the kind of ministry I would want on a regular basis. But so often we have no choice in the matter. By the way, where is Wally?" he asked. "Isn't he with you?"

"Oh, that's another story," I replied. "He came with me as far as Otrukpo mission, then asked me drop him there. He is such a sad case. Simply couldn't handle coming here. Too stressful. Said he would rather stay there and say his prayers. Told me to tell people he wasn't feeling well if anyone asked for him. But why don't you and I get together after this is over and catch up with each other. We have all been invited by the Franciscan Brothers for a palm oil stew meal at St. Peter's College."

Two large military trucks drove onto the field, directly in front of the posts, and out came ten prisoners in black prison uniforms, their hands tied behind their backs, accompanied by a group of soldiers dressed in khaki-colored working fatigues. They lined up and as the trucks pulled away, the military master of ceremonies called each prisoner by name and announced the nature of his crime. Each one was then escorted to a pole by two soldiers. They immediately began wrapping a rope around the prisoner, starting around the shoulders and moving down to the feet. There were no blindfolds.

While this was in process, another military truck arrived and out stepped immaculately dressed soldiers and an officer who took up a position about fifteen yards directly in front of the poles as their truck pulled away.

When I first arrived with my teachers, the military police had directed us to a section of the stadium almost in line with the poles. We were only about fifty feet from the nearest prisoner. I would have preferred to be much further away.

In a voice that clearly indicated he was educated and trained in England, the officer barked the orders. There was an almost a simultaneous bang, a series of flashes, and I saw the nearest prisoner slump against his pole. Although I thought I was following the proceedings carefully, the speed of it all took me by surprise. Then "Fire!" A second volley went off. I jumped again. This time I saw the body nearest me, now slumped against the pole, with blood from his chest spreading over his dark prison clothing, his face frozen in a nauseating grimace. The sound of the bullets hitting human flesh filled me with disgust, shock, and loathing. I silently joined my prayers with those of Jim.

Within minutes, the bodies were removed, the national anthem was sung again, and the Governor exited in his Mercedes.

I had seen many people die from sickness and old age, but to witness life taken away by others, like this, in a public spectacle, I found to be sickening. It brought home to me something that for many years I had not really thought about, something that I took for granted: that I was living, working, and ministering in a very primitive environment.

CHAPTER 6

Obedience

"*Ogaba!*" Joe screeched when I stepped down from my Land Rover parked at the end of the verandah and walked onto the patio, dropping my filthy knapsack with a sigh. "*Igbi! Uche!*" he continued.

The same to you, I thought: *Shit! Damn! Hell!* My gray parrot seemed to take a perverse delight in greeting me with obscenities in Igedde slang. From his point of view, perhaps it's what I deserved after being gone ten days on safari. He bounced up and down in his cage on the wall near the "gin slab," our patio, and jabbered a few more unpleasantries before taking a more civil tone:

"*Obi,* Mike."

"*Obi tchow,* Joe," I replied.

Hello, hello. His excitement spent, Joe fell silent, bobbing his head from side to side as he rocked back and forth on his perch. I was home again.

"Welcome back, Father," hooted Emmanuel, our ancient cook, through his toothless smile. His wrinkled, balding head mimicked my bird as he nodded and shuffled, barefoot, to help my houseboy and bush cook Alfred offload the camping equipment from the dirt encrusted truck.

81

"Welcome, lad," added Wally. My squat, pot bellied boss and house-mate arched himself out of his armchair, holding out a hand in greeting. His left hand, holding a lit cigarette between nicotine-stained fingers, quivered slightly as smoke spiraled up between us.

Sitting out on our patio in the evening, simply relaxing and enjoying a cold beer was a pleasure I always looked forward to. I glanced quickly to the right side of Wally's chair for the line of empty bottles. Seeing none, I concluded that he had just removed the evidence, probably when he recognized the sound of my truck turning onto the long, rutted driveway up to the house. Now he appraised me from head to toe, wincing at my unshaven and disheveled appearance. The red laterite dust of the region, driven from the Sahara desert by the scorching *harmattan* winds infused my sweat-stained clothes. With temperatures well over one hundred de-grees at midday, this was the hottest time of the year; the rains would not be falling for another two or three weeks. The dust permeated everything. It was impossible not to feel it, smell it, and taste it.

"I've missed you, lad," Wally murmured, squeezing my hand. He looked down as my two German shepherds rushed towards me, eagerly circling, licking my hands and legs, barking for attention. I reached down to pet them, ruffling their ears.

"Are you going to take a shower first?" he asked. "Or do you want a beer?"

"Thanks, Wally," I said. "It's good to see you too. I think I'll have a beer first. I'm so thirsty. How've you been?"

"Not bad," he replied. "Oliver!" he shouted over his shoulder to our new houseboy who stood in the darkening shadows of the verandah, cau-tiously watching everything. "Don't just stand there. Bring the Father a cold beer. Come on, lad!"

He waved his hand at my chair. "Then sit down, put your feet up, and relax. You must be tired. Give me all the news from the bush."

Backing up to the easy chair, I collapsed with a loud exhalation and eased my tired legs onto the bloated camel skin pouf. For a split second I felt out of place, as if nothing here were real. Then I was overtaken by a sense of calm as I sank into the comfortable chair. I was reluctant to share what I'd seen recently, suddenly protective of my hard earned intelligence. After all, Wally never ventured into the bush anymore. Ever since a serious auto accident years ago, he had lost confidence in his ability to drive. He rarely left the mission compound, and though he'd been here for ten months, he still hadn't even visited the small village of Oju only a quarter of a mile away.

Safari work – visiting the almost fifty remote outstations in our parish, checking on the construction of schools and clinics, meeting and paying teachers, visiting with school children, saying Mass, and performing baptisms and marriages - was the core of my life as a missionary. This is what I did, and now I was the only priest to minister in this mission, since I was the only one capable of driving and hiking.

Wally placed the small, battery operated radio in its usual place on the low patio wall. Both radio and antenna were positioned for optimum reception. I knew that he wanted to catch the 7 p.m. news on the BBC World Service. He was essentially an organized man with strict rituals. Looking me over with a slight grimace, he spoke softly, "You're probably too tired to talk tonight. Just sit back and rest; there'll be plenty of time to review everything in the morning." Then he jerked upright. "Christ, where's that beer? Oliv----."

Before he could finish, our new houseboy appeared.

Oliver advanced quietly behind my chair, carrying a sixteen-ounce bottle of beer in one hand and a glass in the other. He was a skinny nervous kid, with scabs covering his legs. One of my old T-shirts clung to his chest. He had only been with us for a couple of weeks and hadn't yet adapted to Wally's routine.

"Here, give it to me," barked Wally, as he heaved himself up and reached for the glass and bottle in one effortless movement. He opened the large bottle with one hand while holding the glass with the other, and poured without spilling a drop. *Done like a bartender,* I thought.

"Alfred!" I called to my houseboy who was finishing unloading the truck. Speaking in Igedde, I added, "Take one of the chickens to share with the other boys." It was part of the assortment of hens and ducks we brought home, gifts from the many villages we had visited. This time we had even collected a small goat.

"Yes, sir, Father," Alfred said, smiling. "Thank you, Father."

"You spoil these kids," grumbled Wally. His chair scraped back a couple of inches as he flopped back into it, lighting another cigarette.

"Ah, that's good," I sighed, savoring the coolness of the beer as I stretched out on one of our fine ottomans. The old-timers called them "Bombay fornicators" because they had arms that extended about two feet out in front, and it was relaxing, if a little vulgar looking, to rest your legs on them. A few years ago at St. Peter's College in Otrukpo, I'd seen the college principal, a great raconteur, sharing some anecdotes to the amusement of his guests. Stretching out his legs on a fornicator, he seemed oblivious to the lack of adequate underwear beneath his wide-legged shorts. His manhood was very much on display for his audience, particularly for the nuns seated directly across from him. I wondered ever after whether it was just the principal's stories that held their attention.

Wally's voice drew me out of my reverie. "Leeds lost again last week," he announced somberly, reaching out in an almost robotic manner for his cigarettes on the end table alongside his chair. "What a mess! Can't figure out what they're trying to do. It's very disappointing, lad, very disappointing. I think Don Revie's days as head coach might be numbered. Manchester United won again. Wouldn't be surprised if they win the league. That should make *you* happy."

I smiled wanly and nodded my head, hoping it would pass for enthusiasm. English soccer was the last bastion of passion for Wally. His disabled brother, to whom he was very attached, would send him stacks of sports newspapers that arrived weeks, sometimes months after the events. Nonetheless, he read each paper cover to cover with the curiosity and devotion of a research professor. He was a simple, bluff Yorkshire man struggling to re-create the semblance of the home he yearned for, while living deep in the Nigerian bush, fifty miles from the nearest large town.

"Take your time with your beer, lad. I'm going to have another after I see Africa." Wally patted me gently on the shoulder and walked to the far end of the verandah, where he unceremoniously took a leak while staring off into the deepening night. In a country where running water was precious, I had learned early on, that this was the accepted method of relieving oneself at night. It was Wally who'd labeled the ritual "seeing Africa."

I wasn't sure how many beers he'd already consumed. I was certain, though, of how the night would end like a recurring bad dream that would leave me irritable and depressed.

"I know you enjoy speaking the language, lad," Wally said as he levered himself back into his easy chair, "but you need to be careful with these people. Let's keep it in English in front of them. There are times when I wish I could speak Igedde myself, but you must watch being too familiar. These people need to know their place."

Please dear Lord, I thought, *let's not get into that again.* Wally had never learned any native language during all his years in Nigeria, and even though the Mass had already been translated into Igedde, he still gave the service in English.

The noise of our generator starting up halted his familiar commentary for a moment. Twisting around in his chair, he looked over his shoulder to make sure that the house lights were on, his right hand mechanically reaching out again for his cigarettes.

"You've heard me say this before, but when you've been around these folk as long as I have, you'll know I'm talking sense. Hell, you and I both know that all their brains are in their dicks. Shit! No need for them to dress up for Halloween. All they would have to do is throw their dicks over their shoulders and walk around as gas pumps. And remember what I told you: if you have to take a leak when any one of them is watching, hold it with both hands. Don't want to let the team down," he chuckled wickedly, obviously still amusing himself with an old routine. "Anyway, English is taught now in all the schools, so we needn't be catering to them," he huffed.

Darkness had now completely settled over our little compound. We sat in the shadows away from the house lights since they attracted swarms of insects. I could hear the sound of beer splashing into his glass. I was tired and dirty and wanted to take a shower now, but I knew Wally was just warming up. If I got up and walked away before he finished venting, he'd be terribly hurt and would mope around for days. Once when I'd cut him off, he'd followed me around for the whole of the next day like a little boy looking for signs that his mother was no longer annoyed with him. So like many times before, I decided to stay put and tune out as much as I could. Inwardly I raged: all I wanted was for him to get off his fat ass and do a day's work for a change.

"You youngsters are all the same," he sighed. "What's with you? You think that it's important to learn their language, eat their food, and respect their su-perstitions. In my day we would call that 'turning native.' These people don't deserve that much energy and consideration. It's not too long ago that they were swinging about in the trees. And when they fell out of the trees, they landed on motorcars and bicycles. And I don't believe that they have invented the wheel yet, and isn't that supposed to be the first sign of civilization?"

I yawned and stared back at the old man, too tired to fake an indulgent smile. Speech number one was about to end, but was interrupted by Alfred approaching stealthily on bare feet, addressing me from behind my chair.

"With the Father's permission," he said in Igedde.

"Alfred, come around here where I can see you," I answered in kind. "What is it?" I briefly locked eyes with Wally, searching for any response to my continued insubordination, but he only turned his head to belch and then gaze off into the darkness.

Alfred moved to the side of my chair with his head down to avoid eye contact. The Igedde people did not like to sit or stand in what they considered to be a confrontational position; rarely did they ever look us in the face. Wally and I had had a heated discussion on the subject, after I had found him chastising a houseboy like an English schoolmaster. When the boy turned his face away, Wally berated him even more. I'd tried to explain why the approach was wrong, but it fell on deaf ears.

"My sister has sent word that our mother has had an accident," Alfred said softly. "Since we are not going to bush again this week, I would like to see her and visit with my people."

"Is she badly hurt?" I asked.

"I don't know," he said. "My sister said her leg is very big and sore."

"Of course you can go," I answered. "Why don't you take a couple of days? And please give my greetings to your family. I expect to visit your village later on in the week. If you see Chief Oga Hula of Ojenya, let him know I would like to meet with him also."

Alfred's village was the nearest one to the mission, just about a quarter of a mile away. It was Oga Hula who had given the land for the mission twelve years ago.

"Thank you Father, I will greet them for you, and I will leave in the morning at first light."

He padded away as quietly as he had arrived, his feet making no sound on the warm cement floor. With his departure, I wanted desperately to get away from Wally's habitual rant.

"What's the news on the war?" I asked. "For some reason, my radio wouldn't function when I was in the bush. I must remember to take a look at it in the morning."

"We're still the closest mission to the front lines," Wally said, "but it does appear that the action is moving further south towards Onitsha. It's difficult to know exactly what's happening. I was worried there for a day or two when you were out; all this shit makes me very nervous. You never know, you never know…." His voice drifted off.

"We went over all of this before I left," I replied testily. "I gave you my itinerary. We agreed that you could always send a boy on a bicycle to come get me if there was an emergency. Remember, you could also have sent a message to Jack in Aliade. He would have come and picked you up."

"Yes, yes," Wally conceded. "You're right, lad. You're right. Do you want another beer?"

"No, thanks," I said. I glanced over my shoulder to see if Emmanuel was preparing the dinner table. "I really feel grimy and want to take a quick shower. Will the food be ready soon?"

"Let me check with that lazy bastard," Wally sighed. "He's always stealing food and giving it to his family."

Easing himself out of his armchair, he waddled off into the darkness. One thing he did well was rule the kitchen with strict protocol and a great deal of attention. Food was prepared in a small separate building at the back of the house where our cook worked miracles, including baking bread, using a wood-burning stove. The temperature inside must have been unbearable at times, including tonight.

A short while later, feeling much refreshed after a quick shower and a change of clothes, I walked back on to the "gin slab."

"Cook says it's about ready," Wally said. "Go on in and sit yourself down."

"Aren't you going to eat?" I asked.

He paused for a second, but I already knew the answer. "I'll have another beer right now. I'm not particularly hungry. But you go right ahead. I'll still be here when you're finished."

I glanced around the house; it was immaculate as usual. Wally had the boys well trained and took pride in how the place looked. The painted cement floor had been polished and shone like glass. The furniture had been dusted and not a cushion was out of place. Even the old paperback novels that lay next to Wally's favorite chair, were all neatly stacked, edges together, all facing the same way. The dining room table was beautifully laid out for two people. This fastidiousness was Wally's hallmark; I was sure that every mission where he'd been pastor was maintained the same way. Perhaps this was one area of his life where he felt in total control. It was also one of the few good things other priests had told me about him, before we met. "You won't have to worry about decent food or keeping the house clean," one of them said jokingly. "That is his purpose in life."

Our mission house itself was one of the better ones, built in a very simple ranch style in local red stone. Each bedroom had a shower and toilet, modern amenities which were most unusual in this diocese. Of course, the water had to be pumped by hand each day from our own well, but Wally also took care of that.

And here we were, the only two white men in the region, at the end of a bush road a long way from any significant town, living and working together in an area not yet recovered from a bloody civil war that had torn the country apart.

"That was a really good meal, Wally," I said, walking back outside in time to see him lighting another cigarette. "Thanks for asking the cook to make my favorite groundnut soup. The rice and beans with stewed goat were delicious."

A self-satisfied smile crossed Wally's face, and he nodded. "You're welcome, lad. I do my best to find decent ingredients, but that lazy bastard cook needs a lot of coaching. Come and sit down. Have a beer, or would you prefer a whiskey?"

"No thanks," I answered, "I'll sit with a coffee for now." Wally was already on his way to the refrigerator. Ironically, he was quick to criticize priests who regularly enjoyed spirits; he escaped self-criticism by declaring himself "a simple beer drinker."

Like most night during the dry season, it was beautiful just sitting outside, enjoying the cooling down of the day. There were no sounds of vehicles, only the faint hum from our generator in the background. And then as my ears became accustomed to the silence, the night sounds of Africa started up, penetrating through the darkness: the never-ending chirping of crickets, the high-pitched shrieking of fruit bats in the trees off to the side of us, the occasional cry and burst of laughter from the nearby hamlet, and sometimes the beat of a drum. On these hot dry-season evenings, people frequently danced, and sounds could travel for miles in the still air. We savored the silence for a while, each of us absorbed in his own thoughts.

Then a chorus burst from the shadows: "Good night, Fathers! May God bless you, and may you sleep well." The houseboys and the cook, their chores completed, had silently lined up a couple of paces behind our chairs, in order to give us their customary, final farewells of the day.

"God bless you too. May you sleep well," we both responded in unison.

"Alfred, would you cut the generator, please?" I asked. "And put the bird away."

The generator's hum faded into silence. The house lights behind us dimmed and then vanished, accentuating the darkness. The peculiar dry-season smell drifted through the air, a mixture of burned wood and fresh mangoes. I could now vaguely make out the shape of the tall Igedde hills against the skyline. As my eyes became accustomed to the blackness, they slowly took in the enormity of the African night sky, and I was mesmerized by the sheer beauty and clarity of the stars.

"I hate this fucking place," Wally exclaimed, bringing me back to earth with a jolt, "and the asshole who sent me here." Speech number two had begun, slightly slurred. "It's nothing to do with you, lad. It's this whole shitty system."

Oh no, not again. I thought I had dodged this bullet. Get off your piss-potty, Wally. I am really sick and tired of your belly-aching.

I half turned my head towards him and watched, as even in the dark he unconsciously reached out with his right hand for his cigarettes. He shook out a single stick, the glare from the match briefly illuminating his face, accentuating the lines and creases. I'd never really noticed it before, but tonight he looked quite old.

I sighed with exhaustion, my moment of inner peace shattered. *Here we go....*

"You would think that after twenty-five years I'd be in a nice town parish, somewhere decent. Don't you think I deserve it?" Wally was momentarily distracted by several fruit bats diving and swooping over our heads and ran a smoothing hand over his hair. "Why did that bastard Bishop Foley move me from Otrukpo? He couldn't say it to my face...

had to wait until I was on furlough in the UK… had to make a place for Frank…had to move Frank out of Makurdi because he couldn't stand him either…needed a special parish for one of his young favorites…after twenty-five fucking years."

There was a dull thud as Wally set down his glass. His words were increasingly running together. "Twenty-five years and what have I got to show for it? I've had enough of black men to last me a lifetime. They can't be trusted; they're all thieves and liars."

"Maybe the Bishop will make this a temporary assignment, Wally," I suggested weakly, not knowing what else to say.

"Temporary, my ass," he snapped. "I knew Seamus long before he was made Bishop…. I know too much about him, and he knows it. I'm not one of those who suck up to him. If his appointment had been based on a straight election, he would never have got the job…. I'm sorry, lad. You're the youngest and newest out here. You really don't need to know all this shit."

I didn't respond, wondering if I should simply go to the Bishop and tell him that my pastor was a hopeless alcoholic. Wally clearly needed to be sent back to the UK, but would the Bishop give any credence to me, the youngest priest in the diocese? Probably not, and he might see me as a complaining upstart with little respect for senior priests. In this goldfish bowl of a diocese, that would not be a good reputation to have or to be noted in my personnel file.

Finally, I realized that I should say something. "I'm sorry you feel this way, Wally," I murmured halfheartedly. "That's a lot of shit to handle. But why have you put up with it all this time? What keeps you going?"

I immediately caught myself, regretting my question. If I had been less tired, I wouldn't have made the mistake of encouraging him.

"What a question, Mike…You of all people should know what drives me. If I didn't have God in my life, I would never have managed… I'll get my reward, my satisfaction later… There's a crown in heaven for those who persevere… And then I won't give a shit about those bastards."

"We can leave at any time," I offered, trying to take us in a different direction. "Look what the Spiritan priests did in Haiti. They all walked out, to a man, and they didn't ask for permission."

There was a very long pause; maybe Wally was drifting off, and I was about to suggest that we turn in when he came to life again. "Look, lad.

We're not just priests and missionaries, we are Religious... We belong to an Order... We all have specific vows. Poverty, Chastity, and Obedience... These are not things to be messed with...Took them for life, I did... I came to Africa out of obedience, same as you did... *Obedience*, lad...That's the tough one, simply doing what you are told without question."

I shook my head in disagreement, and then retorted more loudly than I had intended. "Wally, we're not chess pieces to be moved around at the whim of a Bishop. Each of us has to have some say in where we go, and what we do. There has to be a dialogue. If I didn't want to be here for one second longer, then believe me I would request a move, and quickly."

"But that's where we differ, Mike. Most of you young lads look at religious life differently than the likes of me. Didn't you read in the seminary about the saint who was told to plant cabbages upside down out of obedience? And you know the result. They all just grew normally." There was a brief pause. The cigarette glowed more brightly for a second, followed by a long exhalation. His beer glass made a quick, gentle tinkling sound as it knocked against the bottle.

"It's not that I don't want a fucking move, lad. There's not a day passes that I don't think about it. It's simply that I can't ask for one. It would go against everything that I accept as holy. So the bastards will probably leave me here till I rot."

He didn't say anything for quite some time. As he reached into his pocket, pulled out a handkerchief and blew his nose, I guessed he was weeping. I didn't know what to say. Even if I could find words, I wasn't sure I could say them without getting even more irritated than I already was. Both of us just sat there for what seemed like an eternity.

Wally finally spoke in a choking voice, so soft that I had to lean over and strain to catch all the words. "It's getting late; I'm going to turn in. You're a good lad, Mike. You're a good lad, but you have so much to learn. It's good having you back." He heaved himself out of his chair without saying another word, gently placed a hand on my shoulder, gave it a slight squeeze, and then slowly made his bowlegged way towards the end of the verandah. I could hear him pissing into the night, and then the sound of his door closing.

I sat and stewed for a while; I was angry with the Bishop and diocesan authorities. They had placed this man in a bush situation, knowing full well he was badly assigned. Wally had sat on his ass for decades, passed on from one mission parish to the next, doing the bare minimum in terms of ministry to the poor. And I began to think about all those needy people, who could have been ministered to by a caring and effective priest.

A mosquito suddenly gave me a nip on the back of my knee, breaking my train of thought. Another was buzzing around my head. I needed to either turn in soon or get covered with bites. What little comfort I'd felt in returning from safari had vanished. Returning home, had only reminded me that I was very much on my own.

CHAPTER 7

Loneliness

An air of abandonment and decay hung over the mission house of Udei. For about six miles I had been following a narrow, bumpy, red-dirt road lined with trees so tall that they almost blocked out the sunlight. Then suddenly I entered a large circular clearing in the forest. For a moment I was blinded by the glare. A hodgepodge of buildings appeared unexpectedly. On the left side, about fifty yards away, I could just make out what looked like a square bungalow with an old, corrugated iron roof. It was barely visible through the tall elephant grass and cassava plants, and it seemed to be squatting on the edge of the jungle. On the other side of the clearing was a series of structures, clearly identifiable as a school that had once been painted bright red, but now was a dirty patchwork of streaky pink and bare cement walls. It struck me as strange that there were no windows and no doors, just openings where they should have been. The sagging and undulating roofs were made of what looked like scrap metal sheeting, and it appeared that at any minute they would get tired of the struggle to support themselves, and would simply let go and come crumbling down. I would soon discover that this was actually a very fine school with almost nine hundred students, and it was mine!

On the far side of the clearing, centered between two Flame of the Forest trees in full bloom, was a long narrow building with a large cross on the outside wall. I assumed it to be the church and meeting hall. Many years ago it had been whitewashed, but it was now mostly brown, showing me that it was built out of mud bricks.

There was no sign of life. I cut my engine just to listen if I could hear any voices. Nothing. Silence. Not even a bird call. The air was absolutely still. I glanced at my watch. It was almost two o' clock, early afternoon, and in this fierce, oppressive heat I mused, anyone in the area would be resting and most certainly not working.

Tracks where a vehicle had once regularly passed were faintly visible on my left. They were wide enough for my Land Rover to pass, but were now covered in tall elephant grass almost five feet high. I assumed that this must be the path to my future home.

As I plowed my way along the overgrown driveway, my front bumper created a cloud of choking dust that filled the hot air with flying debris, making it almost impossible to breathe inside the cab. I quickly reached for my handkerchief, holding it over my mouth and nose. In the mirror my hair looked as if I had been in a snowstorm. Grass seeds and straw stuck like Velcro to my sweaty shirt.

And suddenly it was over. I found myself in a small clearing that turned out to be the back yard of the mission house. The tire tracks led me directly to the right side of the building where a small, makeshift carport had been constructed with sides of native matting and a roof of palm fronds. It clearly would give shade and protection from the sun. But suddenly I realized it was too low for my truck. I pulled up short and slid out of the cab, at the same time reaching across the seat for my bush hat. It was like stepping into an oven, and in the few seconds I was uncovered, I could instantly feel the sun beating down on my head. A memory flashed through my mind. "So it's Udei, is it?" murmured a caring old timer on learning of my new assignment. "It will either make or break you, and it's hotter than hell. I'll pray that you make it."

"Welcome, Fadda, welcome."

I turned around quickly in surprise at the voice, since I hadn't noticed anybody. Perhaps I was too focused on making it through the elephant grass, and in any case my sunglasses were now completely covered with dust. Peering through my squinted eyes as I cleaned the lenses with the edge of my shirt, I noticed a short, thickset, rather squat man with tear drop nail marks cut into his cheeks, and tattooed cats' whiskers around his mouth. He strolled over from a bamboo cot under the shade of a large cotton tree. Close by was a large, typical, round mud hut with a grass roof, with several smaller huts directly behind it. Hitching up the long brightly colored cloth wrapped around his waist, he rubbed his eyes with the knuckles of one hand and held out the other to me.

"I am Aiyeh, your cook, Fadda, and I would like to know what the Fadda would like for 'chop' tonight."

"Hello, Aiyeh," I said, shaking his hand. "It's good to see you again. How are you and your people?" He rubbed one foot on top of the other. It was a sort of nervous gesture and I noticed he had an old, long scar across his ankle, probably from a machete cut while farming. "Perhaps we can get all my baggage into the house first, and we can talk later about food."

"Yes, sir, Fadda," he responded, and shouted loudly over his shoulder in Tiv. A young bare-breasted woman suddenly emerged from one of the mud huts. Her cheerful face also bore the telltale tribal marks of the Tiv people. Her hair was attractively braided in a unique style called "Benue Cantilever Bridge." She had tied a colorful cloth under her breasts, and as she got closer I noticed that it was supporting a very small baby sleeping on her back.

"Welcome, Fadda. I hope that your journey was not too tiring. My name is Lydia, the wife of Aiyeh. We were expecting you but thought you would arrive later in the week. We had planned to have all the school children clear the road before you arrived."

"Hello Lydia and thank you. Your English is very good," I remarked. "Where did you learn it?"

"In the Sacred Heart School." She waved a hand in the general direction of the dirty pink buildings.

"I'm delighted to meet you," I said, moving towards the house.

"Please, sir, Fadda. Will the Fadda make time to baptize my baby?" she asked.

I was a little taken aback, but in an area where the infant mortality was extremely high, and there had been no priest for almost a year, I knew I'd probably be inundated with such requests.

"Of course, Lydia," I responded. "I'll take care of that just as soon as I'm settled in."

It was evident that the house had been neglected for years. Open yellow shutters lay flat against the walls, the wood dried and cracked. They looked like downcast exhausted pairs of eyes, brooding over the sad heaps of fallen paint flakes on the verandah below. Parts of the interior ceiling had fallen in and hadn't been replaced, exposing the bare metal roof; this made the house unbearably hot. As I stood at the doorway looking into the yard, if it were not for Ayeh and Lydia off-loading my truck, I would have felt that I was in some kind of ghost town. Several of the outbuildings were in a state of near total collapse, slowly being taken over by the encroaching jungle. Unlike most of the newer missions there was no generator for electricity: lighting was provided by kerosene-filled Tilley lamps. Water had to be hand-drawn from a well every day, and the bathroom was clearly an after-thought: a low, small, flat-roofed affair with a fifty gallon drum on top that had once been painted yellow, that Ayeh informed me was filled with water by schoolboys each day. After drawing the water from the well, they then head-carried it up a makeshift ladder to the tank.

To the side of the house stood the foundations and pillars of what was clearly designed to be a fairly large church. They were now almost completely overgrown, and you had to look very closely to make out the shape of the church. A couple of days later as I hacked away at the bush with my machete, I saw that it was actually made out of cement blocks. Why, I wondered, had it never been finished?

Udei was one of the oldest missions in the diocese and had been founded by German priests some fifty years earlier. It was also one of the poorest and most run-down missions, and had the reputation of "breaking men." I didn't learn this until much later. It was also an extremely difficult parish to travel around because there were so few roads. This meant that visiting villages, schools, and clinics could only be done by long safari treks of ten or twelve days. The people, a particular kindred of the Tiv tribe, were not very receptive to any formal religion. The mission had never really developed, and of the three previous pastors, two had left the priesthood and gotten married. The other was my best friend, Jim Brown, whom I had once visited here, but who didn't stay long enough to have a major impact. He was transferred to a relatively new mission at Wannune that had been unexpectedly vacated by Ron Cammack who had been shipped back home seriously sick; this was the same Ron who met me in Lagos when I first arrived. I would never see him again. He died three months after he arrived in the UK at the age of thirty-four.

From where I was lying, naked on my camp bed, a small towel over my stomach, I could see the stars through the open window. And the moon was so bright I could make out its face: I imagined that it was smiling at me. I needed time to think. I needed time to make some fast adjustments. I needed time to figure out where I would start. This was my first parish as pastor. I was now on my own, and had the chance to prove to the Bishop, my colleagues, my family, and everybody else just how good I was. And I was determined to do it. I was thrilled by the challenge, excited by the prospects of turning this god-forsaken dump into a spiritual and material paradise. I would work hard, draw on all my natural resources: my love of people, my planning ability, and my creativity. This was why I had come to Africa. In spite of my impoverished surroundings, I felt rich and happy with where I was, and fell asleep dreaming only good things.

But the day had not started that way at all. My furlough in the UK had been extended by my boss in London, the Father Provincial, who had asked me to help out with a major project in the seminary. He had promised me he would communicate with Nigeria and explain the situation. Unfortunately, he failed to honor his agreement. Arriving back in Nigeria, my best friend Jack let me know "Boy, are you in deep shit. The Bishop is after your skin."

"What the heck for?" I asked.

"Well, Mike, for starters, you should have been back two months ago and apparently nobody let him know where you were. Look, as a friend I suggest that you go to our own boss first and see what he has to say."

I knew from Jack's tone that this was not good and without even waiting for a beer, I drove the hundred and fifty miles to the mission house of our Religious Superior, Paddy Ryan. He lived far into the bush on the east side of the diocese. I arrived in the early evening and fortunately he was at home.

"We've all been waiting for you, and yes, the Bishop is well and truly upset with you," was his opening greeting.

"Well, didn't anybody get a letter from the Provincial in England? Didn't you hear anything?" I asked.

"Look, Mike, I knew what you were doing. I'd heard it through the grapevine, but officially nobody was informed of you being temporarily re-assigned to work in England."

"But it wasn't my place or my responsibility to inform the authorities out here," I insisted. I felt cornered and unsupported. "So what do you think I should do?" I asked nervously.

"You need to go and meet the Bishop and hear what he has to say."

"Well, since you are the Superior of us Spiritans, I would like you to go with me so we can get this whole thing sorted out."

"No, Mike. I don't think that's a good idea," he insisted. "You need to take care of this mess yourself."

"Look," I argued, my irritation and anger rising. "I'm the fall guy here. I have been well and truly set up, and I'm beginning to feel very much unsupported. You could help me fix this. You're my boss, not the fucking Bishop."

"No, Mike," he insisted. "This is your affair, and you need to take care of it yourself."

I was furious, especially with the system over which I had little control. If this was religious life in practice, then it was not working for me. "You fucking asshole," I snapped between my clenched teeth. "You're hanging me out on a limb, and you know full well what will happen. I'm disgusted with you. I can certainly take care of myself, but I expected some support. If this is brotherhood, you can stick it you know where. And if you think I have any respect for you as my boss, forget it. You have the balls of a fly. I'm going to turn in and will be off as soon as it gets light."

"Look, Mike. I can understand you're upset," he said, trying to calm me down, "but all of this is your own making."

"Forget it." I got to my feet. "I'm thoroughly disgusted with the whole fucking set-up, with you, with the English Provincial, and with the bloody Spiritans." With that I stalked into my room. We hadn't had dinner yet and I was really hungry, but food was the last thing on my mind.

On the long road to Makurdi I had had lots of time to run through various scenarios in my head and reflected carefully on the choice of words I would use. Finally, leaving aside my negative feelings regarding the failure of the Spiritan authorities, I was optimistic that I myself could easily resolve the misunderstandings with Bishop Foley. He was not amused to see me drive into his compound in the early evening. As I parked under a tree, then got out of the cab, a white cassocked figure looked down from the upstairs verandah, recognition and thunder written all over his face. I asked the secretary if he was free, which he was, so I went directly upstairs to meet him. There were no greetings as we stood face to face, he behind his desk and me standing directly in front of it.

"So Father Barrington, you have finally deigned to return. How dare you show up in this diocese after abandoning your mission? You have shown a total lack of responsibility and consideration for everybody out here, and I find your behavior abominable, totally unacceptable, and an indication that you have no interest in the work of this diocese."

"My Lord, I'm sure that the English Provincial has explained…"

"The affairs of the English Province do not concern me. You have failed to return after I allowed you to take an early furlough, and your cavalier attitude in taking an extension is without precedent. While we are short of priests, I'm not so sure that there is room out here for your kind." His volume intensified, and I was sure he could be heard all over the compound. All the windows of his office were wide open and a fan overhead whirred softly, but the temperature in the room felt stifling.

"I had assigned you to Udei Mission, and it has been without a priest for many months." Glaring at me and poking his finger into my face, he snapped, "You have prevented those poor people from having the Mass and the sacraments, and it will be on your conscience. I suggest that you take up your assignment without any further delay. You are a disgrace to the priesthood and to the great missionary traditions of this diocese. I have nothing more to say to you. You may go now."

This tirade surprised me, and for a moment I was tongue tied.

"My Lord," I responded, struggling not to show my anger. "I do not deserve the kind of attitude and language you have used. And the comments concerning my sense of responsibility are totally unjust."

"Father Barrington, I have said what I needed to say. You should leave my office immediately."

"Well, my Lord, if that is all you have to say, if that is really what you think about me," I snapped back, my anger now beginning to get the better of me, "then you can shove Udei up your ass since I am clearly not the kind of person you would want there. If you have an issue with my being temporarily assigned back to the English Province, then I suggest that you take it up with the Provincial in England and with my Superior out here, Paddy Ryan. However, since I am such an undesirable, I probably will be taking the next plane out of here." I stormed out of his office, slamming the door as hard as I could.

I was fuming as I jumped into my truck and headed to the central mission upon the hill opposite the Bishop's compound. Running quickly upstairs to the patio where I knew the community would be gathered, I immediately assumed that somebody from the Bishop's house had made a phone call because the priests there were all very guarded in welcoming me back to the diocese. I spoke to them honestly and said I wasn't sure what I would do.

A few minutes later, Eddie Oliver, the new Vicar General arrived and tried to calm me down. Taking me aside, he said, "Look, Mike, I was in my office and I overheard everything. I feel you have been treated very unfairly. But what are your plans? What do you intend to do?"

"Right now, Eddie, I'm too fucking mad to know what I should do." I got up from my chair and walked over to the verandah. I needed to pace, to let some of my anger out. Eddie followed closely behind. "I know what I want, and that's to head off for Jos airport in the morning, and take the next sodding plane out of here."

Holding me by the elbow, he gently slowed me down. "Well, Mike, I'm asking you not to do that, even though I can understand your anger and hurt. You are one of the youngest and brightest priests in the diocese and we need you. You are too smart to let this prevent you from doing what you have always wanted to do."

We paused, looking out over the town. I could hear the thump, thump, thump of the mortars as women prepared the evening meal. In the distance, just beyond the market place where the canoes came in each day with fish, I could see the River Benue, the moonlight turning it into a wide curving silver ribbon. Kerosene lights flickered in many of the small houses below us. A radio blasted out music that I recognized as that of King Sune Ade. A big truck sped by, its gears grinding loudly as it slowed on the hill near the Bishop's compound.

We stood there in silence, each of us with his own thoughts.

Eddie was the first to speak. "There are people out there Mike, who need you. Isn't this what you have always wanted to do? Isn't this what you trained for all of those years? Then don't let this incident prevent you from doing God's work."

I turned towards him, offering a cigarette. He lit mine, then his own. Counseling me to stay, he explained how upset the Bishop was and how I needed to understand the sort of pressure he was under. He assured me that he would speak with him, and would also make sure that the Provincial in the UK was contacted to explain the situation fully. He also said it was most unfair of the Bishop to take his anger out on me when the real issue was between the English Provincial, the Bishop, and my local Spiritan superior Paddy Flynn.

"Eddie, you're right, and just now I'm too upset to make any kind of decision," I said. "I need a little time to think things through."

"Mike," he said, "I'm on your side, and I'm here if you need me."

Later that evening, after dinner, we spoke again and I emphasized that I trusted him to clear up some of this mess. I also agreed to go to Udei the following day. I'd always trusted Eddie and found him to be very fair in all his dealings with me.

This episode with the Bishop created such a rift between us that it was not fully bridged throughout the rest of my time in Nigeria. We would speak when necessary, but it was always with a certain distance. I didn't trust the man. I never received a word of apology from him nor a word of regret about his unjust anger towards me. The Provincial in the UK neither wrote to me nor accepted responsibility for his own behavior. He didn't last as the Spiritan Provincial and was voted out of office shortly after this episode. Although he never did apologize for his behavior and failure to support me, I met him later and shook hands with him. Some people just don't have the guts to own up to their responsibilities, and he was one of them. Knowing that, I moved on.

For my part, I was never big enough to make a formal apology to the Bishop for my choice of language and behavior. In hindsight, I know that I should have done this even if he was not ready to accept it. The experience sowed the seeds of distrust in me and later disenchantment with religious life. Over time these seeds would germinate and would eventually lead me to make a major decision in my life. Despite everything I'd learned about brotherhood and community, when the chips were down I was really on my own. Heading for Udei, even though I would be permanently and physically living on my own, at the age of twenty nine I would also be pastor of my own parish.

I made one stop on the road to Udei at the cottages attached to the local high school where a couple of Peace Corps workers were staying. And it was my lucky day. Eddie Oliver had mentioned that one of the boys who was returning to the USA, had trouble finding a home for his large male German shepherd. His colleague simply did not want to be bothered with the dog.

"Don't worry about it anymore," I said. "I have only one question: will the dog travel in my Land Rover?"

We were all seated in the living room where I had previously enjoyed several parties. Josh, the dog's owner, went over to a table covered with a heap of papers, books, and what looked like the remains of breakfast. Rummaging around for a couple of minutes, he finally found what he was looking for.

"Here, Mike, you can have him," he said, handing over a chain leash. "You'll have no problem with Pev, he loves to ride in a truck."

Throwing myself into my parish duties, I worked long hours, seven days a week. In six months I was never visited by any of my colleagues, and I felt so burdened by the volume of work that I had little time to visit them. But I was isolated and I felt it.

My loneliness was suddenly broken one day by an unusual character, who was soon to become a good friend, and he was not even a Christian. Al hadji Umaru had been to Mecca and had his own small business running two mammy wagons to markets in the Udei area. Not long after I'd taken up residence in Udei, a wagon loaded with goods and people drove into my compound. Out jumped the "wedgy" with a big block of wood to put behind the wheels. My big German shepherd took off barking at him. The kid dropped the block and shinnied up a tree, screaming in fear. Out stepped Umaru, laughing his head off, and telling the boy in Hausa to come down, that the dog would not harm him.

Al hadji Umaru was a youngish-looking man, dressed in a native, two-piece, light gray suit and wearing a beautifully colored, hand embroidered, round *huluna* on his head. I rose to meet him and went through the ritual exchange of greetings, asking about health, family, farm, work, and so forth.

"You surprise me," Umaru said smilingly. "I don't know of any other priest in this area who speaks Hausa, and you manage it well. Where did you learn it?"

"My first assignment was to Keffi," I replied. "I had a couple of excellent teachers, one of them an al hadji."

"Well," he continued, looking me up and down, "you are young and bright; I hope that you remain here a bit longer than some of your predecessors. This mission has a reputation, and it is not a good one."

I was too shocked to ask what he meant by his last remark, but over the next few months, I'd learn a great deal about this man and his knowledge of many Spiritans.

By this time my two houseboys, having heard the wagon and the barking, appeared on the verandah. Umaru greeted them all in Tiv which he spoke fluently and chatted with them for a minute. I tried to talk back to him in Tiv, and he burst out laughing. "Barrington," he joked, slapping me on the shoulder as if he had known me all of his life, "you should give up the Tiv. You speak it very badly."

Switching to Hausa he said, "You should continue improving your Hausa. I will enjoy conversing with you." In almost perfect English he then inquired about Jim Brown, one of the former pastors of Udei.

"Where is he now? He could speak Tiv very well."

"He is in Wannune, and I'll tell him the next time we meet that you are asking for him."

Umaru had heard that there was a new Father in the mission, and had not only come to introduce himself, but to ask if he could exchange a warm beer for a cold one! I was a little surprised since he was a Muslim, but I made the exchange and invited him to stay. He couldn't on this occasion, but later on when I was at home, especially on a market day he would come and spend an hour or so with me. There was an air about this man that was different from anybody I'd met so far: he was educated, sophisticated, and was very articulate. I got to know Umaru to the point where even if I was not at home, he could always enter my house and exchange his warm beer for a cold one. When I needed building materials moved, I used his wagon, which I paid him for, but he would also sometimes bring me supplies from Makurdi for free.

I was intrigued by this man, and one rainy morning when he came for his cold beer I asked him, "Where did you learn to speak such good English?"

"I grew up in the far north where my father was in government service with the British almost all his life. He insisted that we all learn English."

"But did you go to school, or did you learn it at home?"

"My father sent me to a government college after elementary school, and for a brief period I even went to a Teacher Training College. However, I really did not like it and dropped out to join my brother who was starting a family transport business."

"So you have other siblings?"

"Oh, yes, I have a sister and two brothers. All of them live in Maidugri, and one day I would very much like to take you there."

After this encounter, his visits were almost weekly, and I really looked forward to them. One day he unexpectedly insisted that I visit his house in Makurdi. Since this was the center of the diocese, and there were always priests and nuns there on business, I was hesitant to be seen with an al hadji. But Umaru was so persistent I finally agreed on the condition that he also bring me back.

He was delighted. I rode with him in the cab of his mammy wagon as it made stops in the villages, dropping off and picking up passengers and their loads. We chatted with people who were surprised to see a white man, let alone the "Fadda" riding with the "al hadji." Priests were normally discouraged from taking this kind of transport, because the wagons were often in such need of repair that it could be a dangerous experience. At dusk, the wagon was stopped so that all the Muslims on board could set down their mats at the side of the road and say their evening prayers. In Makurdi, after quickly emptying the wagon, he drove directly to his home.

By this time it was getting quite dark. The house didn't have electricity. Bush lamps placed in each room created all kinds of mysterious shadows. The single-story house was downtown, and not in one of the fancier neighborhood. It was, however, quite large and very nicely furnished, albeit sparsely. I was introduced to all four of Umaru's wives whom I could hardly make out as they squatted in the shadows of the sitting room, until he instructed them to prepare a fine meal for me. He was clearly thrilled to have me as his guest. We laughed, joked, drank lots of beer, and exchanged stories.

As each wife brought in her food for us, we talked about the war and politics. He gave me a tremendous description of, and insight into, the Nigerian Muslim world and what it had been like for him to make the Hadj. I asked him about drinking alcohol, and all he said was, "Every man has a weakness, and Allah understands." I was amazed at his breadth of knowledge and his understanding of the Catholic Missions in the area. I was also delighted with his being so unafraid to speak his mind on any topic.

As the night wore on, our discussions lengthened. I was asked about my parents, my sisters, and my seminary training, and he was especially interested in why I had become a priest, struggling to believe that I'd never slept with a woman. He had a great sense of humor and could joke about the holiest of issues, from my explanations of religious life to his lifestyle as a Muslim. After a slight lull in our conversation, he quietly asked me as his special guest if I would spend the night in his house. I was shocked and at a loss for words. For some reason I had a real sense of panic. I think deep down I was afraid that if I said "yes" the priests at the mission, which was just around the corner, would find out, complain about my behavior and accuse me of turning "native." He clearly sensed my hesitancy and laying his hand on my arm gently squeezed it.

"Barrington," he insisted, "You are my special friend, and I am asking you again to pass just this one night in my house." I slowly shook my head but was emotionally really torn inside. Part of me felt that the most natural thing to do was to agree and say "yes." But the irrational was in control.

"I really cannot, at least not tonight," I replied.

"But I am begging you, my friend," he said, turning to face me intently as he repeatedly slapped the back of one hand onto the upturned palm of the other in typical Hausa supplication. "It would be a great honor for my family."

We sat there for a moment in silence, the shadows from the bush lamp dancing on the walls. I was suddenly conscious of the night sounds around me. Through an open window close by a radio was blasting out Nigerian "high-life" music. Male and female voices were raised in argument, or were they merely enjoying each other? A baby cried in the distance. A mosquito hummed near my ear.

Quietly, but suddenly Umaru got up and walked out of the room without saying a word. I wondered if I had really upset him or whether he had just gone to ease himself. A minute later he returned, leading a woman by the hand. As they approached, in the light from the bush lamp, I could see that she was quite young.

"Look, Barrington" he said. "you are my friend; you can even have my youngest wife for the night if you will only honor me by staying." He then spoke to her in Hausa, "Come on, show my friend how nice your breasts are."

Without any hesitation, she reached up behind her back to untie and lower to her waist the colored cloth that was wrapped around her body.

For several moments I was speechless, never having been in this situation before. I was in no way tempted; I was terrified. Struggling for words I mumbled, "Umaru, what are you saying? You know I am a Catholic priest, and we don't sleep with women. I cannot accept your offer."

"Oh, tell me another story," he replied testily. "Men do it everywhere." He spoke in Hausa to his wife and ushered her out with a wave of his hand. I understood that he was telling her she could go back to bed.

"And do you think I do not know which priests are sleeping around in the town even tonight? Do you think I do not know which women regularly sleep with O'Connor and Collins (two Spiritans) who come into town several times a week? It's common knowledge. Every man has his weakness, but Allah understands." I could feel his disappointment with me, even in the dark as he stretched out in his easy chair and called for another beer.

"I don't believe for one-second that a man can go for more than twenty-four hours without some sexual satisfaction, and that includes priests. Allah made it pleasurable so that it could be that way."

I was shocked that he would have such information, and I was also beginning to feel uncomfortable at where all this was heading. I wanted to create an exit strategy but was unsure how. The darkness in the room seemed even more intense and I wished I could see Umaru's face to try to read his emotions.

"Look, Umaru, thank you for the offer, I appreciate everything you have done for me. It's been a wonderful evening, but it's getting to be very late, and I told my catechist that I'd be leaving on safari first thing in the morning."

I knew that he didn't believe me, but he was too much of a gentleman to insist any further. "As soon as you are ready, I would appreciate it if you would take me home."

Awakening his senior wife who was huddled asleep in a corner of the room, he told her where he was going and drove me in a torrential downpour the forty-five miles back to Udei. We couldn't talk much because of the noises from the empty wagon bouncing and sliding all over the pot-holed, muddy road. The mission was in complete darkness as we arrived, but within seconds my half-asleep houseboy, Akum, appeared with a lamp. Umaru and I embraced. I thanked him again for his hospitality and watched from the verandah until his tail lights disappeared into the stormy night.

As I lay on my bed, I couldn't sleep. Thousands of thoughts raced through my head, and I was obsessed with the image of Umaru offering me his young wife.

Had he been joking? Then why would he wake her up and bring her into the room? If he wasn't joking, then how badly had I handled it? Had I lost his friendship because of my refusal? And what about the young woman? There was no question of my sleeping with her; I simply couldn't because of my vows. Even if I had accepted, I wouldn't have known what to do.

I had often fantasized about being with a woman, but I also knew these images were all in my imagination. I sometimes dreamed about being in another situation: a married man, with a loving wife and perhaps children, teaching in Africa. But I knew that this too was daydreaming. At the age of twenty-nine, I had never even seen a woman naked close-up, and I'd certainly never touched or explored one sexually. I'd never dated or gone through the normal teenager and young adult angst of falling in and out of love. My celibate seminary training and lifestyle had excluded any possibility of discovering what sex or a loving intimate relationship could be like.

So my imagination ran riot within me. Could I have consented to sex with an unknown woman, one I couldn't even clearly see, one whom I had never really met? Would it be someone I would like? If I was going to have sex, I would need to like that person. Could I have trusted Umaru that he would never have boasted to his friends about it? After all, he had told me about other priests. And what about the wife? She would surely have spoken about it to the other wives, and then what? It could never have been kept a secret. But what if I were wrong and the secret would have held? What would it have been like? What if we'd had sex and she had become pregnant?

I couldn't sleep. What frightened me? Why didn't I simply stay the night? If I had, how would I have gotten back the next day? There was no market in Udei, and Umaru would have been up early and on his way to some other town. How would I have explained it to any priests who might have found out about it? The Makurdi mission was just around the corner and I would have been sleeping just a few minutes away from a comfortable mission house with all its amenities, instead of in a Muslim household without running water or electric light. How would I have explained it? Perhaps this was my real fear; I wouldn't have wanted to give explanations to anybody about my actions. I couldn't risk their negative questioning or their criticism.

The experience stayed with me for days, and in hindsight I'm still a little saddened that I was unable to accept Umaru's hospitality. I didn't need his wife, but it would have given him great pleasure to have me stay with him as a real friend. I'd somehow failed him. However, he remained the perfect gentleman and continued to call on me at the mission, exchanging his warm beer for cold, and bringing me up to date on the latest political developments. We continued our discussions, and our friendship deepened with each encounter. Sadly, after my transfer from Udei to the other side of the diocese without phone or local mail service, it was impossible to maintain our relationship.

CHAPTER 8

Happiness & Sadness

I knew immediately what was wrong. Being bounced around on the deeply corrugated pot-holed roads, having to constantly wrestle with the steering wheel, was the norm in this area. But this was different. Something was very wrong. As I slowed down and tried to head for the side of the road, it was as if my juddering truck wanted to spin me around completely and flip over. I struggled to remain upright and came to a complete stop. I knew I had a flat tire.

I was on the road from Makurdi to Lafia and only eight miles from Udei but was really in the middle of nowhere. Changing a tire on the side of a dusty dirt road, engulfed in cloud of choking red dust sent up by the trucks and mammy-wagons thundering by, was a challenging proposition. I had just unbolted my spare tire from its cradle behind the cab when suddenly another smaller Land Rover pulled up behind me. I grabbed my handkerchief so as not to breathe in the dust.

"Do you need some help?" As the dust began to settle, a thick set, grey-haired, tanned white man, wearing a very dusty, blue, work shirt and shorts emerged.

"It's kind of you to stop, but I think I can manage," I replied, extending my hand, "but thank you for the offer. I am Father Mike from the local Catholic mission."

"And I am Alberto Tedeschi-Ferlini," he said with a flourish and a smile, shaking my hand with a vice-like grip. "I am the senior mechanic with Borini Prono, the construction company building the new road. I am in charge of the camp about a half a mile back. Perhaps you have noticed it?" His heavy accent betrayed where he was from.

I had wondered what was going on there. A large area of the forest alongside the road had been cleared, and a series of huts was being constructed. I was soon about to discover they were bunk houses, a mess hall and recreation facilities, and offices. There was also a huge mechanics' workshop.

"Please, please Padre, allow me to take care of it for you." He didn't wait for an answer. "You two," he called to the workers leaning against his truck, smoking, "take care of this for the Padre."

"Yes, sir, yes sir," they responded and immediately took over the task.

"Come Padre," Alberto beckoned, "we must sit out of the dust. My Land Rover has air-conditioning." He led the way to his truck, holding the passenger door open for me.

This was amazing. I'd never been in an air-conditioned vehicle since I arrived in the country, but it was a comfortable relief.

"And how will you get your tire repaired?" he asked.

"It will have to wait until I am able to get to Makurdi next week," I replied.

"No no, no, that is too dangerous. It is too long. How will you manage if you get another flat? You will come with me to the camp and I will fix it for you now."

Borini Prono was an Italian company and although they had hired many Nigerian engineers, all the key personnel were from Italy. The road camp was situated about half-way between Makurdi and Lafia, and although Udei was six miles into the bush, technically it was in my parish. Adolfo was not just the senior mechanic he was also the general foreman for the camp layout.

Several weeks later I met with him again. I had called in just to say hello. "Buon giorno, Adolfo," I yelled in greeting above the din. There was a massive earth-moving machine rumbling past, and I was leaning out of the window of my truck. He had his head buried under the hood of a small pickup.

"Buon giorno, Padre, what brings you here? Are you having more trouble?" he asked, turning his head sideways. Straightening up, he arched his back, gave it a little stretch and ambled over towards me, wiping his grimy hands on an oil-stained rag attached to his belt.

"No," I responded jokingly, "just wanted to check on my parishioners."

He gave a huge smile, followed with a big belly laugh. On my last visit, he had told me that most of the Italians at the camp were either communists or Catholics who did not go to church. They worked seven days a week for about ten months, spent the rest of the year with their families at home, then returned for another tour. This was a bachelor camp. There were no married quarters.

"But how is the work progressing," I asked as we strolled over to the shade of his workshop.

He paused for a moment, leaning against the shovel of a huge bulldozer, his brow furrowed as he pondered his answer.

"Padre, perhaps you can help me. We have a water shortage. The source we were originally given by the local chiefs has proven to be inadequate. I need water and lots of it, and I need it quickly. We could draw it from the Benue River, but it's not central enough. Do you know where I might find some locally?"

"As a matter of fact, I might have a solution for you," I responded. "Let me check out a few things and I'll get back to you."

An interesting fact of life in the bush was that when the British built the railways in Nigeria, their purpose was not to serve small towns. Their sole object was to transport goods and materials from the north to the coast in the south so that they could be shipped to England. It was all part of the rape of the colonies. Not a single railway line ran east to west. However, the locomotives burned either coal or wood and needed water. Small stations were developed all along the line whether there was a town or not. What was important was a permanent source of water. Udei was one of those water sources.

The Udei station had its own water tower served from two perennial and copious natural springs, more than enough to meet the needs of Borini

Prono. Later that afternoon, I met with the village chief and laid out my ideas. If the chief would allow them to use the water, I would negotiate with the company to construct a permanent road into Udei, all six miles of it!

Quickly summoning a group of elders, the chief asked me to present my plan. "But how will they carry away all the water," asked the old chief, Tor Iyorhembe?

He was sitting on a low three legged chair that gave him the appearance of squatting, and was wearing the traditional hand woven, black and white striped blanket and pointed cap of a senior elder. His long spear rested on his right shoulder, the two feet long blade sticking into the hard mud floor. He looked extremely fragile with sunken cheeks accentuated by his many tribal markings, and his skinny arms looked like crumpled brown wrapping paper. When he smiled, which he did quite frequently, he showed his filed teeth, a practice that was fast disappearing in Udei. However, his was an important voice in the chief's council, and I needed to pay deference to him

"That is a big question, Iyorhembe," I replied. He had never seen or probably heard about a water tanker, so I improvised. "I'm sure they will figure out how to do it: they are all engineers and have been to school to study these things."

He was satisfied. The council voted in favor and asked me to talk with the Italians.

That evening, I drove over to the camp and gave Adolfo the news. Early the next morning, he brought two other engineers to calculate the water flow and its capacity. They were delighted with the results.

Within three days, the old road had been completely graded and a fleet of earth-moving equipment and mechanical shovels was tearing out a ten-foot section of jungle making the road wider. Every couple of hours, a water tanker rolled by, until after a short while the novelty had worn off, and the school kids and villagers no longer stopped and clapped each time they saw one.

Adolfo also was happy. I met him one day close to the mission with his mobile mechanic's team servicing the huge bulldozers and scrapers.

"Come over and have a cold beer with me," I said. "My house is just a couple of minutes away." He had passed the house many times from the road, not knowing that it was the mission. When he saw it close up, he was shocked and wondered why I lived in such poor conditions.

"Money, Alfonso, money! I don't have any to spend on the house. This is a poor area, and the people are poor. We all live very frugally."

"Yes, Padre, that is why you must come to the camp and have a good meal every week. But look at this house. It is a shambles. It is almost falling down. The engineer who built it did not know what he was doing. Look," he said getting up from his chair and touching the sitting room wall, "there is not a straight line in the house. You have no ceiling, no electric light, no power, no air-conditioning. Padre, I had no idea that you lived like this." I hadn't the heart to tell him, that the house had probably been designed on the back of an envelope by a simple priest who just needed a roof over his head and had it built with local, unskilled labor.

"And what is that?" he said, looking out of the window and pointing to the foundations of the church, now overgrown with vegetation, only a few pillars remaining visible.

"One day it will be a church," I said standing beside him. "Another priest started to build it some years ago, but never had enough money to finish it. It too will just have to wait."

"No, no," he replied. "I need to take a closer look." I called for Akom, my house-boy to bring a machete, as we walked out into the blazing sun. He cleared the bush away from one of the pillars so Alfonso could get a better look.

"Padre, this will not support a roof, watch." And with that he began to push and shove it until it wobbled, broke off at the base, and tumbled down in a cloud of broken block and cement dust. "See, there is no steel reinforcement. If this is our parish church, then we must build it correctly. Can you have the entire bush cleared away by tomorrow so we can take a good look at it?"

I was completely taken aback. Did I hear him correctly? Did he say "our church?" Were the Italians going to build me a church?

The next day Alfonso arrived with an engineer who spoke almost no English, but specialized in bridge construction. Together with an assistant, he took measurements of the structure and checked the depth of the foundations.

"Padre, you must come for dinner to-night so we can explain everything."

"OK Adolfo," I replied, both excited at the prospects of a having a church, and yet very nervous about any costs that I would have to cover. I ran the parish literally on a shoe string budget. We even took apart the layers in empty cement bags and sold each one separately, so my house-boys could help feed themselves. It looked like these Italians had no worries about money at all.

I was seated at a table in the big mess hall, enjoying a cold beer, surrounded by a small group of excited Italians, all looking at the plans for the new church. The design seemed very simple, two hundred feet long and forty feet wide, with open breeze block walls, but it was very functional. The church would hold over six hundred people. Alfonso interpreted for me, as the engineer explained that he would tear out everything, including the foundations, and start from scratch.

"Out here," said the engineer, "the big guys have to take care of the little guys." Work would start in the morning, and they would provide all the labor and materials. The rowdy group cheered and shouted their approval while I sat there in shock and amazement at their generosity and kindness.

For the next five weeks, eight hours a day, heavy machinery tore up and graded the ground, and trucks arrived on schedule carrying cement and blocks. I watched in amazement at the speed of construction. My parishioners were thrilled, and took turns, village by village, to bring food for the workers. The old men, including Tor Iyorhembe, would come daily and sit in the shade on my verandah, drink beer, and survey the development with pride and wonderment.

"Barrington, you have done well," he said one day as were sharing a beer. "You should let me get you a wife so you can settle down and stay with us. Your children would enjoy this church."

Coming from an elder who had at least a dozen wives, I took this to be a great compliment, but I told him I was not yet ready to marry.

Opening day was truly wonderful. The Bishop came to bless the church and gave a great speech, thanking the Italians for what they had done. Seven of them showed up for the occasion, and I joked with Alfonso,

"I told you that I would drag you all back to church one day. And today you all attended and even got blessed by a Bishop."

There was native dancing such as I had never seen before, as different performing groups arrived from even the most remote parts of the parish.

The elders killed two cows for the occasion, and both Alfonso and the engineer were presented with the robes of an elder and inducted into their special circle. We all got to witness a very rare event of the Tiv people, a Kwagh-Hir, 'a thing of magic,' a whole night of storytelling acted out with huge puppets and music. It was simply enchanting. Dawn was breaking when the bleary-eyed and somewhat inebriated Italians, who had been plied with copious amounts of palm wine and native beer, decided that they needed to get back to the camp and prepare for another day's work.

Shortly after the church opening, I fell sick. I knew immediately that it was a bout of malaria, and so I attempted to doctor myself. Four days later I was having trouble breathing, with pains in my back and chest. I realized that something else was happening to me. I was really sick and still had a raging temperature. Driving fifty-five miles to Lafia, I called in at the mission where the priests informed me that a new Egyptian doctor had arrived at the local hospital and was very helpful. It took him just a few minutes to give me a diagnosis.

"Father, you have a serious case of pneumonia. I want you to stay here so I can treat you properly," was his opening comment. "It is very common with the aftermath of malarial fever, and it also means that you were not taking good care of yourself."

Leaning against the examination table, the doctor watched me through his horn-rimmed spectacles change back into my sweaty clothes. He was probably about my own age, but tall and slim and very casually dressed in light brown slacks and an attractively embroidered native shirt. He had a disarming smile, spoke perfect English with a very slight accent, and looked as if he was a gentle person. But what I noticed most were his hands: they were so finely boned they almost looked feminine.

The hospital was characteristic of those built by the British in this area - a series of low squat buildings around a central courtyard that once was grass, but was now bald and brown through the trampling of thousands of feet. A broken terra-cotta fountain that had seen better days was its centerpiece, and was now being used by a local woman as a makeshift kitchen where she cooked and sold cassava and chicken. Iron sheeting, once painted green, covered the roof, and the faded-blue walls and verandah pillars were stained from the constant touch of thousands of dirty hands, and sweat marks of people leaning against them. As I walked

115

from my truck, the first things to hit me were the smells: disinfectant, stale urine, and open sewer. In the hospital compound, hundreds of people were milling about, many of them in small groups around small fires and flimsy make-shift shelters of sticks and sheets of blue plastic. In my sick state of mind, I couldn't help but think it all resembled a scene from Dante's Inferno. These were the families of patients from the bush who came to care for their loved ones. This was where they lived, sometimes for weeks; this was where they cooked. No form of sanitation was provided which accounted for the overwhelming stench. The hospital itself provided no food or bed coverings; these had to be provided by the families. There were no free medicines, not even for emergency care; these had to be purchased separately.

There was no way I could stay here. The sights, the smells, and the noise alone would make any normal person sick. But the doctor insisted, "I have a separate room that is only used by government personnel; you will be just fine there."

Reading my negative reaction correctly, he emphasized just how serious my condition was.

"But how about if I stay at the mission and come here every day so that you can see me," I said stubbornly.

He thought about it for a minute.

"The priests there are my good friends," he replied, "and if you agree to stay there, I will give you the medication, but you must rest, you must stay in bed. Bed rest is crucial. I will come each day and check up on you."

Five days later my fever was gone completely, and I was beginning to feel a little better. However, I really needed to get back to Udei. Several of the boys from my parish had passed the entrance examination for the seminary, and I had received a message that Steve McLane was coming to my place to do the interviews. I had not had another Spiritan stay with me in more than two years, so I really wanted to be there. Against the doctor's wishes, but with my grateful thanks and a pocket full of streptomycin, I drove home.

Some days stick in one's mind, and this particular Sunday was one of them. I had arrived home the previous evening and was so exhausted that I went to bed without even taking all my clothes off.

It was very early when I awoke. Lying there, I could already feel the humidity rising and knew that we were in for a really scorching day. Through the open windows, I watched the fiery sun slowly heave itself up from the horizon. Its rays, shining through the gently waving branches of the palm tree close to the house made a million flashing patterns like a giant magic lantern show. It felt good to be home.

I stretched out my arm from under my mosquito net, reaching for my cigarettes on the night stand. The packet and my lighter were there just as I had left them before my trip to Lafia. I flipped open the packet, only to find that it was empty. My first reaction was to summon Akom and ask him to go to the market and buy me another pack, but something stopped me. It was as almost as if I heard an interior voice saying, "Don't do it." I thought about where I had just been. Here I was recovering from malaria, recovering from pneumonia, still having some trouble breathing, and I was craving a cigarette. I was trying to kill myself. It was insanity. I didn't hesitate. I crunched the packet in my hand, and lifting up a corner of my net, I threw it out of the window. Rolling on to my back, I made a promise to myself that my health would always have top priority. I never smoked a cigarette again nor did I ever crave one.

Steve arrived that night. He was from my home town, so we had lots to talk about, and I enjoyed his companionship. He had fully recovered from his broken neck. It all seemed so long ago now, but it happened on the day I first arrived in the diocese.

"So what's all the news?" I asked? "Let's sit out for a while so you can give me the latest; then I suggest that we turn in early. Tomorrow will be a long day and we both need our beauty sleep."

"Scandals everywhere," he joked, as we were sitting on the verandah, enjoying a beer under a crystal clear, moonlit sky. The silhouette of the new church stood there, regally impressive in its symmetry and simplicity; the light from the moon reflecting off the silver aluminum roof, cast an ethereal glow across the compound.

"One of the Bishop's secretaries, the blond girl from Wales, is pregnant," he continued. "The Peace Corps teacher at the Trade School is the culprit, I hear. Rumor has it that they will get married in a couple of weeks, and then head off to the USA. His Lordship is well and truly pissed since he paid for her to come out here and she will not be able to complete her contract."

"I have no idea who you are talking about, Steve. Living alone out here I get no news, and rarely go into Makurdi. And when I do, it's only a brief visit so I can pick up mail and supplies. But it sure sounds like some folks are having fun."

"Then you don't know about Simon Adasu," he continued. "It's a very strange case. As you know, he was one of the first native priests to be ordained in this diocese. You yourself were there last year for the big celebration."

"Yes, I was."

"Well, he has already quit, gone, taken off, and vanished into thin air," he said, emphasizing his statement by clapping both hands together. "Poof, just like that. Gone." I sensed that Steve liked to be dramatic.

"Nobody is sure where to exactly. He was an assistant in Taraku parish and was able to partially empty one of the parish bank accounts prior to departure," he said sarcastically," but thank God, Tony Duffy the pastor, was smart enough to keep control of the others."

"Wow, that is a surprise," I commented. "I am shocked. So soon after his ordination; what the heck happened?"

"Well, apparently the diocesan authorities didn't do their homework. He has had a wife for several years, and has three children. Apparently it was common knowledge in and around his home village, but word of it never reached the seminary or the Bishop's house. The authorities are still trying to figure that one out," he said with a laugh. "They think he's headed for Lagos where there's a large Tiv community."

"And on that note, Steve, why don't we head off to bed? And oh, by the way, you don't need to worry about anything in the morning; Akom will take care of you. There should be about fifteen kids to interview, if my memory serves me, and they will all be at your mass at 6:30 a.m. I'll see you at breakfast. Sleep well."

"Sleep well yourself, Mike, and God bless you."

Interviews for entry into the junior seminary took place just once a year, and there were always far more successful applicants than places available. Steve had been teaching at St. James's College for five years. Of medium height, with a suntanned face and a very wiry athletic body topped with a mop of unruly black hair, he looked the epitome of health. Once he donned his white cassock, it was almost like looking at a missionary picture postcard. He was four years older than me, extremely intelligent, and from what I had heard, an excellent teacher.

Although my house was not ideal, Steve thought it was the best place for the interviews. The visitor's room was already set up as a bedroom-study, but he thought that using the living room would be less formal and less intimidating. I agreed, not thinking any more about it; after all, he was in charge of the process and had done this sort of thing all over the diocese. I left him to handle everything and said I would see him at lunch time.

My plan for the morning was to meet with a group of my teachers and go over the new religion curriculum that had recently been distributed. Many important changes were taking place now, ever since the Bishop had started a Development and Training Center for lay church leaders in Gboko. In addition, it had already started producing new texts and translations.

Walking down the driveway towards the school, I was totally preoccupied with how I would present some of the class material. The kids were outside having their assembly, complete with school band, and looked so European dressed in the same red uniforms: dresses for girls, shirts for boys. I waited for the headmaster to get to his office and was about to ask him how he planned to organize his staff, when I realized in my distraction with getting Steve situated, I had left my personal notes in my room.

"Augustine, I am so sorry," I began speaking to the headmaster, "I need to go back to the mission for my folder. I'll be back in fifteen minutes."

"It's not a problem Father," he replied, "it will give me a little more time to be with my staff."

Not wishing to disturb Steve, I slipped in unnoticed through the back door and was surprised that there was no one in the sitting room. Thinking that perhaps Steve was writing his notes, I quietly walked across to the visitor's room. The door was slightly ajar.

"Steve," I called entering the room. "Are you...?"

I was completely dumfounded. Akom, my own houseboy was lying naked on the bed, and Steve was handling his genitals. Akom looked confused and alarmed.

"Steve," I said, trying to control my voice, "would you please come to my office."

"Akom," I said gently, turning away so that he would not be embarrassed, "please get dressed. Your interview is over and I will meet with you later."

"I need an explanation, and I need it quickly," I stressed, grabbing my desk chair and staring at him. I was furious. "How could you, how dare you, do this to any kid, let alone a potential future seminarian? What the hell is going on?"

"Mike you don't understand. There is nothing wrong. We have to be sure that the kids are the age they say they are, by checking if their testicles have come down. This is simply routine."

"For God's sake, Steve, please don't try and cover it up. You know what you are doing. You know what this is. Why did you need to touch anybody, to touch Akom at all? You can see that he is a young man and well developed. He is sixteen years old, I have his baptism certificate. I know his mother. I know when he was born. He is growing a beard! How much proof do you need?"

I couldn't believe how unfazed he was with my outburst. Sitting quietly in front of me, he calmly lit up a cigarette, gave me a half-wry smile and said, "You are completely out of touch with things. The seminary is not the same as it was when you were there — how long ago was that, four or five years?"

I was out of patience and struggling to put all of this together.

"Ayeh," I shouted, getting up and looking through the open window to the cook sitting and working outside the kitchen, "would you kindly go and tell the headmaster that something has come up and I will have to re-schedule our meeting."

"Yes, Father," he responded, and took off jogging towards the school.

"And you," I turned and pointed a finger at Steve, "will continue with the interviews in the sitting room, and I will be there with you. There will be no more discussion until they are finished. Then we will both go back to the seminary."

"It's so nice to see you, Mike."

I had just pulled up in front of the priests' house at the seminary near Makurdi, and Barney, my old boss, as pale as ever and squinting in the sun, but with a big broad smile was walking down the verandah steps to welcome me.

"Come on in, come on in. I take it you will be staying for dinner?"

"Hi, Barney," I said, then turned around to get a better look at the new compound. The seminary had moved here from Keffi a year ago and this was my first visit. It was beautifully laid out with freshly painted, multi-colored buildings, young flowering shrubs (no doubt Barney's handiwork), and a startling new and very modern college chapel as the centerpiece.

"It looks like you are going up in the world," I joked, "and yes I will stay, and I would like to have a private discussion with you if I may?"

"Absolutely, absolutely," he responded and led me into the house.

I had decided just as soon as the interviews were over what my course of action would be. Steve told me that there were several other parishes on his schedule and wanted to be in Korinya later that evening. I was adamant, however, that he drive back to the seminary immediately, advising him that I would follow him, since I wished to discuss the situation with Barney. In spite of his protestations, he realized I was deadly serious.

It felt so good after a shower and change of clothing to sit in a comfortable air-conditioned room, and enjoy the relative luxury of it all. It was only a fleeting feeling, but I was a little envious of the amenities. We were seated across from each other in deep comfortable arm chairs in his office, sipping cold beer. I knew immediately from the tone of his voice that he had not yet had time to ask Steve why he had returned so early, or if he had that he must have been given a quick and deceptive answer.

"Well, then, how can I help you, Mike?" Barney said, after we had finished our small talk.

Picking my words very carefully, I let him know that I needed to share some serious issues and related in detail everything I had seen in the bedroom, the explanation I had been given by Steve, and why I had insisted he come back. I knew that Steve's explanation of his actions was not seminary procedure, but I asked Barney about it anyway.

It was as if time stood still for a long period, but was probably only a few seconds. The face on this very simple, but holy priest registered complete shock and horror as if witnessing some gigantic tragedy.

"Oh, my God, my God, my God," he kept repeating. "Oh the damage, the horrible damage to these young souls...and for how long...and just how many?"

I think he was close to tears. There was another small pause as he composed himself, removing his glasses, rubbing his eyes, and then looking up to heaven as if for guidance. He shook his head from side to side in sheer disbelief.

"I will go to the Bishop first thing in the morning and discuss this with him," he murmured quietly. "Steve will have to be transferred. But Mike," he asked, leaning forward towards me, with an expression like that of a distressed father over a sick child, "what about the kids at your mission? Will you be able to take care of them?"

"I hope so," I replied a little unsurely. "My houseboy trusts me. I would like to think I can help him get over it, but this is completely new territory for me also."

Steve did not show up for dinner that night, apparently claiming that he was not feeling well. I was happy about that, since it enabled the conversations and general discussions to flow freely. Several months later, I learned that he had been sent home to the UK and would not be returning.

Some years later while on furlough, I visited the junior seminary just outside of London, and had not really thought about Steve since that awful day in my house. But there he was, as large as life, teaching young boys again. I refused to speak with him. It was very frustrating and shocking to discover that the authorities were not taking this man seriously. Even though I made my voice known again, and they clearly knew his history, for their own particular reasons they placed him where he could potentially do even more damage.

However, some parents and students finally took action on their own. Both Steve and another priest who had been in Nigeria with me were finally convicted, found guilty of pedophilia, and served time in one of Her Majesty's prisons.

CHAPTER 9

Success and Failure

*T*he drumming had been going on non-stop for days. At first I thought nothing of it; after all it was the dry season and people often liked to dance. But this was unusual. The sounds were different, much deeper and longer, and the drumming was almost incessant. Turan was deep into the bush, very close to the mountainous border of Cameroun; this was my first visit and I knew virtually nothing about the place. The remoteness of the region, cut off by a river that had no bridge and was only crossable in the dry season, and its dense jungle and hilly terrain made any access a severe challenge. Occasionally over the years missionaries had tried to gain a foothold in the region but with little success. I had only met one Christian from that area and he was a teacher, Thomas Akusu.

Thomas' father, Shangev Akusu, had been recruited years ago as a load bearer by the British District Commissioner when he was trekking through this area. Akusu travelled with him back to Gboko, the Administrative Headquarters sixty miles away and remained ten years in his employment. Thomas was born there, and since there was no government school the Commissioner recommended that he attend the local Catholic elementary school close by. Akusu later returned home to Turan, leaving Thomas in the hands of the priests who adopted him as one of their houseboys. They paid for his education through college, and after graduation Thomas returned to his native region to become the headmaster of Jato Aka School, which was on the campus of the new mission and my house, fifteen miles from his father's compound.

We had halted for the night in Akusu's compound where we drank too much palm wine, his wives feeding us like kings. The crystal clear sky, ablaze with a million flickering luminous stars like some giant gossamer mantle, provided a backdrop to the gently rocking limbs of the towering trees above us. A zephyr of a breeze, unable to penetrate the torpid humidity and heat below, was a portent for a night where sleep would not come easily. Although it was almost eleven o' clock at night, and the sun was long gone, there was no need for a fire.

"Thomas," I asked earlier as were eating, "why is there so much drumming, yet your own people are not dancing?"

He ignored my question.

We were seated in Akusu's reception house, a large circular thatched-roof structure surrounded by a low two-foot high mud wall, which could easily hold thirty people. Other than forked poles supporting the roof, the space above the wall was wide open. It normally would have made the house a little cooler, but not tonight and the old man had kindly insisted that I set up my camp bed here. Akusu's house was now quite crowded as the villagers, knowing that a stranger was present, had waited for us to finish our food before silently squeezing in.

In all his years with the Commissioner, Akusu had never learned English, other than a few phrases. My Tiv, however, had become quite fluent and we conversed easily together.

We were relaxing in native easy chairs which were rather like deck chairs, except the cloth was made from unbleached wool, with intricate Tiv patterns from naturally dyed threads of red, green, and blue woven into it. The night sounds of crickets, fruit bats, frogs, and the occasional screech of a monkey surrounded us like some exotic jungle symphony.

"Akusu," I asked, looking at what seemed to be a hundred pairs of little eyes caught in the glare of my Tilley-lamp, peering at us out of the darkness, "are all these your children?" I already knew the answer for

Thomas had already told me. What I really wanted to get to was the topic of a possible school for the area.

He nodded. "I have many wives and they continue to help me," he said proudly.

Unexpectedly, a cock started crowing just behind us. Akusu immediately looked over towards the corner, lifted a hand, and young boy about twelve years old came out from the shadows and knelt at his side. He leaned in closely as the old man whispered something. Then taking two more children with him - I couldn't tell whether they were boys or girls – he hurriedly vanished into the night. A few minutes later he was back. Approaching Akusu from behind, he whispered something, but this time I overheard what was said: "It is done." The old man nodded appreciatively, and the child receded into the darkness.

Speaking in English, I asked Thomas, "What has been done?"

"Oh, it is nothing really," he said laconically, "the kids have taken care of the cock."

"You mean they have killed it?" I asked in amazement.

"Sure. My people live very close to nature. Cocks are supposed to help them get up in the morning so they can go to their farms, not sing at night. This sort of thing happens all the time."

As I looked at the three of us, I was struck by the anomaly of the situation. Thomas was dressed in a bright red, short sleeved, sports shirt and wore shoes without socks. Akusu wore a loincloth and had the traditional, homespun black and white striped blanket of a Tiv elder thrown over one shoulder. I was dressed in a khaki bush shirt and shorts with sandals on my feet. All the adult young men wore loincloths, the women were topless, and all the kids up to the age of puberty were completely naked, except for some of the girls who wore a small string with cowrie shells across their loins.

How does all this fit together," I asked myself? I was a white man surrounded by black people, obliged to communicate in a second language, and I could very easily die or get seriously sick if I did not take special precautions. I was educated, sophisticated and a world traveler, spending a night with a primitive people that just killed a cock because it did what cocks do best! It was as if I should not have been there, and yet in a weird sort of way, in spite of the incongruity, I felt comfortably at home.

My thoughts were suddenly disturbed by the loud beating of a drum that sounded as if it was just feet away. I jumped. Everybody scattered.

"What is that?" I asked Thomas, leaning forward. "Why has everybody vanished?"

"They are sending on the message we have just received, and it is not a good one." He turned to his father and whispered to him in Tiv for a few minutes. "My father says it is fine for me to share with you about all the drumming you have been hearing. I know that you have been curious about it."

"Well, yes," I responded. "It has been going on for days."

"There is a very large village about two miles from here on the other side of the hill and bad things are happening there. They are my people, my father's brothers; I know them well. Two days ago, a very powerful chief, Achenga Adzo, died. He was more than a chief; he was a 'witch doctor' and had great power. People believe that he could turn himself into a bird at night and fly to other compounds to do harm. Even people from far away were afraid of him."

He paused as his father got up and excused himself. The old man wished me a good night and told me I could have anything in his house; then he walked off, not to his sleeping house that was next to this sitting room, but into the forest.

"And does your father believe that?" I asked incredulously, wanting to hear more.

"Of course he does," he replied without any hesitation. "What you have been hearing are the big talking drums telling all the villages in the area about the death and the funeral arrangements. Only certain people know how to beat the drum correctly; every village has its own drummer. When we receive a message, we pass it on to the next village and so on until they have all received it."

"So what is the latest news?"

"They cannot bury the chief until all the elders and other medicine men have gathered for a council, and until they have somebody else to go with him. He is a big chief, so he needs a companion even in death."

"So, what do they do?" I queried, trying to take make sense of it.

"In the old days, they would send out warriors to people we did not like, to other tribes like the Jukun, and they would come back with a couple of heads. The message we have just received said that the funeral can now take place, so they must have another body. That is where my father has gone. But that is enough for one night; I am tired and we have a long trek in the morning."

"You are right, Thomas. Thank you."

The drumming continued throughout the torpid night, and my head was so full of questions making their own noise, that even with the physical fatigue sleep was out of the question.

As we were enjoying a coffee together, in the "reception room" I asked, only half expecting an answer, "Well, Thomas, did you find out any more about who else is being buried?"

He looked as if he too had not slept and I didn't dare to enquire if he had gone with his father to the ceremonies, but I suspected that he had. "Yes, of course, but I knew that last night. It's Achenga Adzo's first wife. She was dancing around the corpse and apparently dropped dead. Everybody is saying just how fitting it is to have her go with him."

"What," I exclaimed incredulously. "You mean she actually dropped dead in front of everybody?"

Thomas gave a sort of hollow laugh as he stood up and threw the dregs of his coffee into the bush behind him. "Father Mike, in these situations, nothing is natural. You are in the heart of Turan and things happen here that even I do not fully understand. She was poisoned, of course, but she was also a very old woman and it was her time."

I did not know what to make of all this, and I found Thomas's almost cavalier attitude somewhat disturbing. The early morning air was cool; in fact it felt a little damp. It would not last long since the sun was already coming up, but at this moment was unable to penetrate the dense jungle. A chilly wave swept over me. We needed to get moving.

"Jacob," I called to my new houseboy who was sitting on the half wall listening to the conversation, "please pack up all the gear, I want to get home before nightfall."

I needed to gather my thoughts. This was my new parish and I was discovering something that was way over my head. I had occasionally heard such things alluded to when speaking with old men, but none of the priests who had worked here had mentioned anything like this.

My curiosity, however, remained and I had one last request. "Thomas, is it possible to see the talking drum?"

"Of course," he responded, "the drummer will be flattered that you asked to see it. It is very close to here, near what we call our marketplace."

A short walk on a well worn path, past the houses and kitchens of Akusu's six wives, led into a small clearing in the forest. On the far side was another small group of mud houses almost identical to those of the old man, and I immediately saw it, just as the drummer started to hammer out a message. Now I understood why the sound travelled so far; it was almost deafening close up.

Located under an open grass roofed shed and resting on a cradle about eighteen inches off the ground, was a six feet long cylindrical drum that was about four feet in diameter. It was simply a section of a hollowed out tree trunk. There was a long uneven slit across the top for almost its full length. Thomas explained that each side of the slit was made of a different thickness so that various notes could be produced like the human voice. The drummer, a young man probably in his early thirties, had an exceedingly muscular upper body, but very skinny legs. We waited for him to rest, and then we greeted each other. He stood to the side, holding what looked like two large inverted and solid wooden hand bells. He beamed with pleasure as I touched the drum, running my hand over the polished wood.

"We keep it under its own shed," Thomas continued, "so that it will not be spoiled by the rain or the sun. It is cared for by the drummer like a child; it must not get damaged in any way and especially not by insects."

This was all very interesting, but I was still struggling to digest all the information about the funeral as we trekked back to my truck. What the heck was I doing in this area, what was I achieving, what kind of ministry was this, traipsing around remote villages, simply "being there"?

It all had started ten months earlier with an unexpected request.

"Father Barrington, I would like you to open a new parish in Turan."

I was sitting next to Bishop Foley in his upstairs office sharing a beer. The relaxed atmosphere of the meeting surprised me, since the letter I had received asking me to report to the Bishop's house, had sounded and looked very formal.

"It's an area that needs to be evangelized, established, and developed. I have been delighted with your work in Udei. You have the language skills and are developing quite a reputation as priest committed to working in the bush. I think you are the best person for the job."

"I need somebody who is a man of the people," he continued, "to take on this difficult challenge. Less than fifty percent of the villages in that area have any Christians and there is a pocket near the mountains that is still — let me use a word that I know may not sit well with you — 'primitive'. Are you willing to accept this new assignment?"

Wow, is this for real? I asked myself. The last serious conversation we had in this office was not pleasant. What an about face!

"Thank you for this opportunity my Lord, and for your confidence in me," I responded honestly; "I will give it my very best effort."

"Excellent, excellent!" he cried jubilantly, leaning over to shake my hand, "I felt certain you would agree." Then walking over to a large desk in the center of the room, he retrieved a white envelope. "Here are your assignment papers," he said, offering them to me. "This venture is close to my heart; I have prayed about it for a long time, waiting for the right time and the right person."

I was a bit taken aback by the Bishop's confidence in me, but I was thrilled with the challenge. I was stumped for words.

This was every priest's dream: to actually start my own parish... This truly would be my time, my opportunity.

My daydreaming was interrupted as the Bishop continued. "Be prudent and cautious how you go about the remote villages there. They are not a priority. Focus on the centers and get yourself well informed before you establish a permanent base."

"And what will be the name of this parish?" I asked.

There was a pause as he reflected for a second, closing his eyes as if in prayer. Then with the faintest shadow of a smile said, "Well I think it would be appropriate to name it after yourself."

"Surely not St. Mike's, my Lord?"

He laughed out loud. It suddenly struck me then that this man was a real human being, and that this was the first time I had ever heard him laugh.

"I wonder if there is such a Saint's name." He chuckled again, his protruding stomach shaking like a large plate of Jello. "And I'm not so sure what Rome would make of it. However, I think it is fitting to call it St. Michael's Parish, Jato Aka. I have already taken the liberty of informing Father Ted Walsh in Adikpo that you will be staying with him until such time as you have your own place ready, and he will work with you to get set up in the main village. Currently Turan is part of his parish. I expect you to be there by the first of the month."

Lunch was interesting since four of my colleagues had arrived on business, and the conversation was lively and loud. It changed somewhat when the Bishop announced that I was to open the new parish. It was as if they had all been challenged. Each one in turn began boasting of his own accomplishments; so many people baptized, schools built, clinics under construction, outstations developed. Stupidly I took the bait, announcing that I hoped my new parish would become a model for the diocese.

The most senior of the group, Pete Griffin, a wonderful priest and after twenty-six years in Makurdi Diocese, a seasoned missionary, leaned over the table and said laughingly, "You're still a kid, Mike. Keep your mouth shut and your bowels open and you will do well out here. Look you haven't even got your knees brown yet." *(Hadn't I heard this so many timed before? And it never ceased to touch a raw nerve in me.)*

Everybody laughed, except me.

I would show them and all the other priests in the diocese just how capable I am. Mine would be the best-organized, the best-developed, the most innovative of all parishes. Its formal opening would be the greatest in the history of the diocese!

"This is Stephen Tarkende, my assistant; he will show you around and help you get settled in. Unfortunately I need to take care of some urgent business in town. I'll be back in time for dinner. Make yourself at home, Mike, you are very welcome here."

"Thanks a lot, Ted," I replied. We were standing in the doorway of the Adikpo mission house that was to be my temporary home for the next few months.

"I'm really pleased to meet you, Stephen," I said, offering my hand, "you probably don't remember me, but I was at your ordination last year, along with a thousand other people. Is this your first assignment?"

"Hi, Mike, it's great to finally meet you. Your reputation precedes you," he said warmly."

He had a nice firm handshake and a great smile.

"Yes, this is my first parish; I've been here almost two weeks. I'm excited about being here and hope that you will give me some coaching.

When I heard you were to open the new parish in Jato Aka and would be living here for a while, I was thrilled. You may not recall, but you were invited to give a presentation at the seminary a few years ago entitled 'ministry in the bush,' and it was thought provoking and inspiring. Your emphasis on being a 'man of the people' caused quite a stir. And Ted was telling me that you also speak Hausa and Igedde fluently as well as good Tiv. I'm impressed!"

"You're very kind, Stephen," I replied, "I'm sure we will work well together."

He was a fairly tall, well-built young man, probably about twenty-six or seven years old and spoke English with just the trace of a lisp. I learned later that as a child, he had had received surgery for a hare-lip, although the scar was scarcely noticeable. He was of course, a Tiv and only the second native priest in the diocese. Like most of the males his age, he bore no tribal markings.

There were only the two of us for dinner, Ted and myself. As we sat outside on the verandah having a drink beforehand, I began to get to know him a little. I had, of course, met him from time to time over the years, but we had never spent any quality time together. He was one of a small group of Irish priests in the diocese that included the Bishop, and they tended to socialize together when the opportunity arose. One thing I already knew about him was that he had left his mark on several parishes as a dedicated and very capable pastor. He was a great builder and had several projects in hand, including one near Jato Aka. It was a school that later I would need to complete.

"It's nice to have someone to talk to," Mike, he said, "I've been on my own for so long."

"The feeling's mutual, Ted," I replied, "and this approach of the 'one man parish' can be wearing. I struggle with loneliness constantly, but what else is there? We are after all, human beings and we need to be with somebody. But there are simply not enough priests."

A young man on a bicycle was traveling past on the driveway thirty yards away and greeted us in Tiv. It was one of Ted's teachers. Beer glass still in hand, Ted walked to the edge of the top step and called him over. For a few moments they conversed and I was impressed that he could handle the language so well. He had been a missionary in Nigeria for twenty years, all of that time spent among the Tiv people. As the man left, Ted turned and rested his butt on the low pony wall.

"You know, Mike," he began, gesticulating at me with his hand holding the glass, "and I want all of your support on this, I'm already having trouble with Stephen. I came home the other day and he was entertaining a bunch of people, mainly teachers, and they were drinking my beer. I want to put a stop to this right away, so I have decided not allow any more alcohol in the house."

Holy God, what kind of stupidity is this? I thought he was supposed to be a well balanced person.

"Well, Ted, it's your parish and you're free to do as you think best. I will certainly comply, but I also happen to disagree with you. What don't you like, the people in the house, sharing your beer or both?"

"Sarcasm doesn't become you, Mike. It has never been the tradition out here to have locals in the house and certainly not for a drink. If Stephen has to meet people he can do it where you or I would, in the office. He is not a Spiritan; he belongs to the diocese, so he has his own stipend from the Bishop." There was a pause as he walked over to the end table next to his chair, re-filled his glass, and waved it again in my direction. His stern face was locked in a grimace as he continued, "We need to be ready for these Nigerian priests. They will need some handling."

This is nonsense and a big assumption. Get with the times Ted. I love to have people over for a beer and a meal and have done it for years. And where the heck does your opinion of the native priests come from? Are you afraid of them?

"I could not disagree more, Ted. These guys are young and inexperienced and have no models other than ourselves. Shouldn't we be the ones to mentor and support them? But hey, he is your assistant not mine, although I wish he were."

I needed to move out of Adikpo, even though I didn't have a permanent house. There was no way I could focus on establishing a new parish while living forty-five miles away. The local community in Jato Aka gave me three small rooms which they thought were wonderful, but the building had a metal roof. The heat was insufferable so I quickly moved into a large mud hut close by, using the other house as a storage area. Jacob cooked our meals on three stones under a low grass shed. Without a refrigerator, whatever was cooked had to be eaten right away. My toilet was a hole in the ground inside a tiny mud hut. For a shower I set up native matting in the form of a square and jury rigged a water bucket with a string. It was all very basic, but I was excited and thrilled just to be there.

Designing my own house was fun and easy to do and I immediately set about getting it constructed. Since most of my provisions were still in Adikpo, in the beginning I generally spent one night a week there. On one such occasion, Stephen was out on safari and Ted and I were together checking the building supplies, when a messenger arrived with a note stating that Stephen was sick with malaria.

"What do you make of that, Mike?" he said sarcastically, "My little Tiv priest wants me to bring him home." Before I could respond, he continued, "Well, he can stay just where he is. He is a local boy and he can get native medicine in the village."

Inside the storage shed the temperature, which must have been well over one hundred degrees was almost unbearable. Dark sweat marks blotched our shirts in gradually increasing, irregular patterns like the work of a modern free-style artist. Perspiration slowly dripping from my nose landed on my inventory list smudging numbers and details.

"Ted, people die from malaria," I exclaimed in disbelief. "If it was me out there, what would you do? But let's get out of here to somewhere cooler where we can discuss this rationally."

"There's nothing further to discuss," he snapped, with a tone that indicated total finality as he walked towards the door.

"Ted, we have a small problem here," I began as we made our way to the house. "Stephen is a brother priest and needs help. I simply cannot stand by idly and do nothing. This is just not right."

He opened the refrigerator and helped himself to a cold bottle of water and a drinking glass from the tray above. I was desperate for a drink, but I also wanted this issue to be settled first. Dragging a chair from the kitchen table, he flopped on to it as if he was dead tired.

"Look, Mike," he said wearily, "if you feel so strongly about him, then you go and take care of him. I certainly will not."

I could not believe what I was hearing and was beginning to be angry at his stubbornness. All of this seemed to be so out of character for such an apostolic priest.

"Then, OK, I will."

"You look like shit," I joked with Stephen, "I hope that you didn't try native medicine."

"No, Mike," he replied with a wry smile, "but what are you doing here, where is Ted?" I had parked under the shade of a large mango tree at the entrance to the village, and hearing the sound of my truck he had come out to see who had arrived. The clammy feel of his hand told me immediately that he had a fever. And why would he be wearing his white long robe on a scorching hot day when he was not ministering?

Once we were back on the road, he shared with me just how difficult it was living with his pastor. There was no trust between them, almost no guidance being given, and he felt dismissed and belittled. Communication between them was strained to the limit. He was completely dispirited and depressed.

"Do you want me to talk with Ted?" I offered. "I would be happy to do it?"

"No, no," he quickly interjected, "that might only make things worse. It's kind of you to offer and I know I can rely on you. But no." He was so edgy and jumpy I wondered if there wasn't something else he was not sharing.

"Then you only have a couple of options, Stephen," I said. "You can bite the bullet and ride this one out. The Bishop will probably move you around parishes fairly frequently to give you a variety of experiences. Or you can ask the Bishop for a move now."

Even under his dark skin, I could see that he was not well, that he was struggling to keep it all together. His eyes were bloodshot and he looked very close to tears. This young man was in pain.

"Mike, I really feel your support, but I cannot ask the Bishop for a move. This is my first assignment and I cannot afford to mess it up. Ted and I had an almighty blow-up just before this safari and it was awful. I was afraid he would report me to the Bishop."

"You are correct in that," I replied. "Then you must make the best of things. If ever you need a shoulder to lean on, you know where I live."

Three weeks later I was back in Adikpo and Stephen was no longer there. Ted informed me that he had been transferred to Korinya mission. It was only much later at the opening of my own parish that I learned the truth from Stephen himself. Ted had asked the Bishop to re-assign him, complaining that he was too difficult to live with.

While I was in Adikpo, I approached the Holy Rosary Sisters to see if they would consider starting a mobile clinic in my parish and was surprised at their positive response. Over the next month we met several times with the local chiefs and elders, and settled on a small market area called Butande, about five miles past the new mission site. It was, not surprisingly, a huge success in an area where the nearest health clinic was fifty miles away, even though the nuns only visited once every two weeks.

Once my house was built, I sometimes tried to arrange to be home on a Thursday so that the Sister on duty could take a small break, have a cold drink, and make use of my facilities. Then one day a new Sister arrived, Terry Shields. I had met her briefly at the convent some weeks previously, and had joked with her about being the only American in a group of Irish women.

We struck up an instant friendship. She was extremely well read and trained in the new theology of the Second Vatican Council and its approach to mission. More importantly, in an area where obtaining serious reading was at a premium, she was regularly able to get publications from the States which she passed on to me. She was also different from the other nuns in her convent. She was in her mid thirties, tall, pretty, and very Spanish looking. In the evening when she removed her veil which she often did, she showed her long jet-black hair. She was a very spiritual and reflective person and a great listener. I always looked forward to her visits

"Father, Theresa Yornumbe is trying to die. Please come quickly." My catechist was banging on my door as I was having a late lunch.

Telling my boys that I would be back later, I jumped into my truck, heading to her small home next to the marketplace. It was crowded with women and I recognized all of them. They were from the church choir and Theresa was their leader. She was lying curled up in the fetal position on a metal bed pushed against a small window so as to catch the breeze.

"What's up, Theresa?" I asked. I could see that she was awake and alert.

"Father, I have been bleeding for two days and it will not stop. I have taken native medicine, but it is not working. Will you take me to the Sisters in Adikpo?"

"Of course," I said, "but what about your husband? Is he home?"

"No Father, but my brother here will tell him when he returns from his journey."

Two of the women agreed to accompany her, and I felt sorry for them sitting in the back of the truck in the dust, as we bounced our way along the pot-holed narrow bush road.

Sister Terry was on duty when we arrived and as luck would have it, an intern doctor from Ireland had just arrived. It took just a short while to get the diagnosis. She had an ectopic pregnancy and needed immediate surgery. It was now almost dark, and the nearest hospital forty miles away across the bush was still under construction, but at least we knew it had a doctor, Father William Golli. Bill, as he liked to be called, was probably the most amazingly gifted priest I have ever met. Born in Poland and ordained a Scheut Father, he dedicated his life to ministering in China. After just two years, he was discovered and expelled by the Communist government. But not to be outdone, he then studied to be a civil engineer and later re-entered China in that capacity. As the Church was forced underground, he continued to be an engineer by day and a priest at night. Discovered once again, he was expelled for a second time. But the call of the mission was so strong, Bill studied to be a doctor and eventually became a general surgeon. Managing to enter China once again, he ministered to the people both physically and spiritually. He was finally expelled again after spending a brief time in prison. Bill eventually found his way to Nigeria and to the Diocese of Makurdi. It was fortunate for Theresa that he was on duty that night.

"Come in, both of you," he yelled from behind his mask, "I'm just finishing off a C-section."

Sister Terry and I moved just inside the operating room doors.

"What brings you here at this hour? I suppose its business for me. So tell me all about it."

Terry read from the chart and gave him a summary of what had been done.

"Great," he said, "she'll be next up; then I'll call it a day. Terry, would you scrub up so you can help me. My assistant here is falling asleep on her feet." He nodded to a very small young woman in full surgical attire standing next to him. "I keep having her eat cubes of sugar, but I think she is done for the day. Oh, and I will need blood since we have no reserves here. Did she bring a relative with her?"

Bill was notorious for the number of hours he spent in surgery each day — at least twelve, I was told. The three Canadian nuns who ran the hospital loved him as a priest but struggled with him as a surgeon since they were stretched to the limit providing post surgical care.

The staff nurse poked her head into the operating theater. Bill was now sitting on a chair, his hands held away from his body. "Don't touch me," he said to me with a big smile; "I'm sterile and I don't want to have to scrub up again. So what is it?" he asked the nurse.

"Her blood type is O positive but we don't have a donor."

"Well, I'm O positive," I said; "will mine be okay?"

"Sure it will," he replied, "go and get it drawn then you can come back and watch me."

I had never been in an operating theater before and I really did not want to witness a surgery. I was convinced that I would pass out if I saw a scalpel.

"Please come this way with me, Father." It was the staff nurse signaling with her hand that I should follow her.

I was led into a tiny room adjacent to the theater containing a small chair and an examination table.

"My assistant will be soon be in to take your blood. Please sit down."

He said his name was Gabriel, which I thought was oddly fitting for the circumstances, and that he was a trainee nurse in his final year. He looked terribly young, but I was hopeless at estimating the age of a Nigerian anyway.

"Before I take your blood, I need to first check that it is O plus." And with that he opened a small kit on the table, pricked my finger, took a small sample, and gleefully announced after mixing it with some chemical, "Yes, you are indeed O positive. Congratulations."

I was not sure what to make of his last comment, but I let it pass. I was very tired and the night was not yet over.

"Now make a fist and I will begin," he instructed me. "You will feel just a small prick."

And with that he proceeded to put the needle into my vein.

"But shouldn't I be lying down," I asked anxiously.

"Don't worry about it," he replied; "I can manage just fine like this."

The next thing I remember is wondering what I was doing on the floor with the assistant holding my head.

"Father, are you all right? Don't be alarmed, you just blacked out. You are fine. Rest for a moment, then I will help you lie down on the table."

I felt anything but fine and my confidence in him was fast evaporating.

When I arrived in the operating room, Bill and Terry were busy at work.

"We wondered where you were," he said. "Are you okay? The nurse said your blood is fine but that you weren't feeling well."

"No, I'm fine," I lied, "I just caught some air, that's all."

I couldn't bear to see what they were doing so I stood with my back to the wall and just prayed for all of them with my eyes closed, losing all track of time.

"Well, that's about it. She should be just fine," Bill announced not talking to anyone in particular. "Why don't I get out of these scrubs and you can come with me on my rounds, Mike; then we'll go and have a bite to eat."

The steady beat of the main generator hushed into silence turning the hospital into darkness. An air of peace and healing settled over the compound. Bill appeared with a huge flashlight, followed by Terry holding a smaller one.

"Let's take a quick peek at Theresa," he said, "then I'll do a fast tour of today's cases."

"I need to go and get some rest," Terry said, "so I'll see you after breakfast, Mike. I'll be up at the convent." We were at Theresa's bedside and Bill and the staff nurse were conversing about the after care.

"Okay," I said. "Thanks for all your support. You were truly wonderful. Good night and God bless you."

"You're welcome. Good night." And with that she walked away into the darkness, her shadowy figure silhouetted against the bobbing light in her hand.

It took another thirty minutes before Bill was satisfied that all of his patients were comfortable and he was ready to go home. Home was of course, a small ranch-style, well appointed but cozy bungalow close by the main hospital block that had its own small generator.

"I'm having a gin and tonic, Mike," he announced, walking over to a low dresser in a corner of his sitting room; "what's it for you?"

"I'll stick to beer, thanks."

"You know this must be what it sounds like in heaven," he mused, his head back, eyes closed as he sank down into an easy chair, his bare feet resting on the low coffee table in front of us. He had put on an LP and we were listening to the Brahms' violin concerto. "Do you prefer the Beethoven," he asked innocently. Unwittingly I said "No, the Bruch is my favorite." I was immediately treated to an erudite expose of the essential differences between all three of them, while also comparing the merits of Tchaikovsky and Dvorak. That in itself was unusual given the setting, but it was also one-thirty in the morning and we had not yet had dinner. My head was spinning and all I really wanted to do was sleep.

Food did eventually arrive and the meal was memorable for the education I received about surgery for hiatus hernia. I unfortunately let Bill know that my father had been diagnosed as having such a condition and in seconds he produced a coffee-table sized book complete with gory, colored surgical diagrams. He was in his element, explaining things like volvulus and fundoplication, even though the text was in German. He casually informed me that in addition to English, he also spoke fluent Polish, German, French and good Mandarin. It was almost three a.m. when we finally turned in and Bill would begin his rounds at seven after saying mass for the sisters, the start of what for him was just another average day.

Theresa recovered in time for the grand opening of the parish. It had taken me almost two years of constant, non-stop, grueling work to get established, but now it was there for all to see. I had designed and built my own house, planted out a whole compound with flowering shrubs and fruit trees, finished building the grade school, constructed a large but simple church capable of holding six hundred parishioners. It was as one priest commented, like "something off a picture post-card." Four other schools and a clinic were in process. I had brought the Sisters into the area. Baptisms and Marriages were recorded in their hundreds. I had trekked the bush from A to Z and visited every corner of my parish and established more than forty outstations. I had spent weeks on end on safari letting everybody see that I was the pastor of Jato Aka.

The Bishop was delighted, complimented me in front of many of my colleagues who had travelled long distances for the celebration, and praised the way I had gone about my work. It was a thrilling moment and I finally felt that "I had arrived."

Two days later after all my guests had departed, I was sitting alone on my verandah in the quiet of the evening, looking at the beautiful hills on the Cameroun border fading into the dusk, when a feeling of great sadness came over me. Far deep within me a voice that I did not at first recognize, was crying. Tears started coursing down my cheeks, slowly at first, then as I recognized the voice, they turned to sobs and I could no longer control them. The voice was my own and it was telling me that I was lost. Who was the real Mike? Within myself I could see Ted the builder, Jim the preacher, Gerry the architect, Alan the planner and organizer, Dennis the linguist, but I could not find myself. I was both terrified and lonely.

I have no idea how long I sat there. All I can remember is that the front of my shirt and my shorts were wringing wet, and I began to feel cold. Rest brought no sleep or respite. I was dogged by the feeling of being in black hole with no escape. For two days I moved like a zombie, and I knew that I needed help, but from whom? I did not feel I could share anything like this with Ted, my nearest neighbor. But then I remembered Sister Terry. It would be her turn to visit the clinic at the end of the week and I decided to take the risk and confide in her.

She was a great listener, and slowly and patiently helped me not only see who I really was, but enabled me to accept and live with myself. Over the next several months she used her skill and her caring to help me put all the pieces together. Through her friendship and insight I realized just how my own ego had blinded me and taken control of my life and that in fact I did not need to compete with any other priest. We prayed together a great deal, becoming true, genuine friends. As the weeks passed, the quality of my ministry changed and my priorities dramatically shifted. But on those evenings when I sat out under the stars relaxing after a particularly busy day, I allowed a powerful feeling that for the most part I had kept suppressed have its own time for review. I was really lonely and after six years of it, I was tired of living on my own. Terry was the first woman I had had any serious relationship with, and eventually because of it my life would change dramatically.

CHAPTER 10

Brotherhood

"Okay, Mike, you're up." It was Jack, calling me from the upstairs patio. He was finishing Vin Mitchell's haircut.

"Thanks, I'll be right there. Just give me a second. It looks like the rain is coming, and I need to get the canvas cover on my truck."

Getting a haircut was not a simple thing. It required a considerable amount of planning — having the time, finding the person who could do it, traveling, and possibly having to stay overnight somewhere. I had heard of priests out here cutting their own hair, but I was not one of them.

I'd arrived at St. Michael's College an hour ago with a Land Rover fully loaded with fresh food and building supplies. With its beautifully laid out campus, this was a great place to relax. I decided to have a beer and lunch, and take advantage of one of Jack's many skills. He was not just known as a sociable and generous host, but he was one of the few priests who knew how to give a decent haircut.

"Alfred," I called to my houseboy, "let's get the supplies covered. The rain could be here in a few minutes." I had been carrying the canvas top rolled up and lashed to the inside of the tailgate for about a week, ready for just such a moment.

"Quickly, now, let's roll it out, and then drag it over the frame. You take the far side, and I will handle this." It should have been simple and straightforward.

"Holy God," I shouted, jumping away from the tarp and holding the index finger of my left hand, "something bit me." It was on fire, as if someone had stuck a red hot needle into it.

"Father, it is a scorpion," said Alfred, seeing the small creature scurrying away on the gravel driveway, "and it is a bad one."

In a flash, he picked up a white-washed rock the size of a melon that was being used as decorative flowerbed edging, jumped around me, and threw it in one lightning quick movement. There was a smile of victory on his face as he very slowly crouched down to retrieve his missile and gingerly picked up the offending creature, holding it at arm's length with the tips of his finger and thumb. I don't know whether it was just the size of his large hand, or because my vision was somewhat blurred by the pain, but the scorpion looked so very small and harmless. His face quickly registered concern, however, as he saw me doubled over and grasping my wrist. If there was poison, I did not want it traveling up my arm.

"Hold that carefully, Alfred," I urged. "How bad is that kind?"

"It's very bad, Father, but it will not make you sick. It will only be bad for some time."

It was just this kind of vague and ambiguous, but well-intentioned Nigerian explanation that occasionally drove me nuts. I understood that he was using a second language and was doing his best for me, but I needed to know in a hurry what specific treatment I needed.

We were all standing. gathered in the sitting room and examining the insect, still in Alfred's fingers, when Jack thankfully gave the verdict.

"This is one you don't have to worry about seriously, Mike," he announced, and I could sense the relief in his voice. "They are common enough in this area, although God knows where you picked this one up. What you need right now though is to cover the finger with ice. You should be okay in a couple of hours." And then reverting back to his old cheerful self, said, "Shit, I wouldn't have known what to do if you had gone into anaphylactic shock anyway. It clearly would have spoiled my lunch."

By the evening my finger was almost back to normal, though still a little swollen and very tender. I decided to stay the night. The rain had moved in, and Jack and I were alone and ready to sit down and have a beer. We needed to catch up on each other's news.

"Jack, I hate to bother you, but do you think you could give me that haircut you promised?"

"Let me get my things; I may as well do it right now." Jack responded, walking over to a long low dresser in a corner of the room. "I always keep my stuff handy."

"Do you want me to trim your beard a little?" he asked, when he was almost finished.

I hesitated for a second. "Well, fine, but if you are going to use the clippers, please go easy near the upper jaw on the left side of my face. I have been having trouble for a couple of weeks with a tooth back there, and quite frankly, I've been wondering what to do about it."

"Not you too," said Jack. He quickly and gently finished my haircut and trim, and called for his houseboy to come and clear up the mess. "I've been having problems too for the longest time and don't know what to do. There's no dentist anywhere in this area anymore. They all ran away once war broke out. I'm living on aspirin and paracetamol right now, and I am getting very concerned. I've really got to take care of myself."

He moved over to the record player, put on an LP of Frank Sinatra, and stretched out in the easy chair opposite me, his crossed ankles and feet resting on the low table between us.

I was always able to enjoy it here, but the electric light, air-conditioning, excellent food, and many other "home" comforts always felt just a little strange to me. I didn't envy Jack; it was simply difficult for me to adjust to these amenities so quickly after living in the bush for so long.

"I have half an idea," I announced suddenly. "And it might be a partial solution to both our problems."

"It had better be a good one," he retorted laughingly." I don't want one of your witch-doctor friends getting his hands on me."

"No," I answered, "I'm not joking. This is worth a shot. The other day I heard from one of my teachers that a dentist had arrived at the Baptist mission at Igbudu, deep in the bush way over on the other side of Tor Donga. These guys are so lucky. They have their own small planes to bring in supplies, and move personnel in and out. No slogging it through the bush for them. It's a long ways away, but I could send one of my boys there with a letter to see if it is true and if we can get some dental care."

He leaned forward earnestly in his chair, and for the first time I could almost see the pain in his face. Jack was physically very strong and fit, and so his response and serious tone somewhat surprised me.

"At this point, Mike, I'm almost desperate. I really would appreciate anything you could do."

It took another four weeks to put the trip together. We had received a positive response from a Dr. Joe Karloski. He would be happy to see what he could do for us. If we could give him just a couple of days notice, he would keep his schedule completely free for us. I sent a boy back across the bush, letting him know we would arrive the following Friday.

Logistically, it was almost a foolish undertaking. Jack lived seventy miles west of Abwa where the Spiritans operated an agricultural college. I lived almost the same distance away but in the opposite direction. Since neither of us had ever been to the Baptist mission and it was not on any map, we estimated it was about a hundred and ten miles away from Abwa, the place we agreed to meet.

Strangely, we both arrived in Abwa almost simultaneously on the morning of the day before our appointment; we had a cup of coffee with Bob Sherwood, the college principal, and then left together in my Land Rover. Mine was the only truck with a four wheel drive, and we would certainly need it. Our goal was to reach Wukari mission, the last Spiritan outpost in the diocese and spend the night there. We estimated that would put us about forty-five miles away from Igbudu, but we had also been told that the dirt road was in terrible condition.

We left Wukari at first light with a fine rain just beginning to fall, and two hours later we reached the mission compound. Dr. Joe, having heard the sound of my truck was waiting for us at the door of a nicely painted, small bungalow surrounded by a well maintained garden, complete with white picket fence. He was a tall, grey-haired, well-groomed man, probably in his late fifties. He was the personification of the laconic Texan, and his sense of humor set the tone for the day.

Once we had finished introductions and met his charming wife, Helen, he asked, "Well, shall we get started, gentlemen? Who wants to be first? And oh, by the way, just so you don't think I will try and proselytize you once I have you captive in the chair, you should know that I received all of my dental training in the Jesuit program at Creighton University in Omaha, Nebraska." His drawl made it sound like "Oomaarhaar." "I think I am somewhat open-minded," he added with a laugh. "What I'd like to do first is examine both of you. I need to know what the problems are."

"Then let's see just how well they trained you," said Jack, moving forward as Joe held open the door that led into what looked like a very well-equipped clinic, "I'll be your first victim."

The news was terrible. Jack needed seven fillings and an extraction. I needed three fillings and the extraction of an impacted molar since that was the tooth causing me the pain.

We went back to the sitting room, and Joe began reading ominously from his notes, "I'll do my best to save the rest of your teeth once I've done the extractions," he intoned gravely.

"Both of you gentlemen have been living on a very poor diet and have given little care to your teeth. This is the result. I'll work with you first, Jack, if you don't mind, since it will obviously take longer. Both of you understand of course, there is a degree of uncertainty in my evaluation since I do not have the benefit of an x-ray machine, and I may run into other issues once I begin. This looks like being a marathon session. If you get tired of me working on you, please let me know at any time, and we will both take a break. Just signal by raising your hand. It's new territory for me too, working like this."

We both assured him that we clearly understood and that he should proceed.

"Mike, please make yourself at home; there are books and a radio over there," he said, waving his hand in the direction of a nice-looking, but locally made bamboo dresser. "There's also lemonade in the refrigerator, so help yourself."

Joe worked with us all day assisted by his wife, who as we found out, was a trained nurse. His technique sounded simple when he described it: "I'll work from the back of the mouth and then do one section at a time."

The Karloskis were absolutely wonderful. Once he'd completed Jack's treatment, they took a small break, and had a snack and a cold drink. Jack could not talk or handle any food at all. Then it was back to work, this time on me.

Once it was over, we sat there, resting for a while in that cozy sitting room with the rain now pouring down in deafening torrents on the metal roof. It was difficult to talk above the din. Helen kindly offered to have the cook make us some soft and light food, but we both refused. Neither of us could face putting anything in our mouths. Added to that, we also needed to get back to Wukari mission for the night, since the longer we delayed, the more chance there was of getting stuck on the bush road. Knowing that we had to leave, Joe carefully and painstakingly went over the dental hygiene plan we should follow. Fortunately, he had the very latest drugs on hand, including antibiotics, and we left armed with everything we needed. We expressed our very sincere thanks and made ready to head off into the jungle. It would be dark within a couple of hours. We wanted to leave a donation for the work of the Baptist Mission, but they would have none of it.

"Who knows," Joe said with a smile, as we shook hands with them both and stepped out into the storm. "We might come knocking on your doors one of these days. We are all doing God's work out here. And I would hate to think, that when I reach the pearly gates, I'll be accused of messing up the teeth of two priests. But there you go," he let out a real belly laugh, "I guess I could blame it on the Jesuits."

We were in too much pain to laugh with him.

Looking back on that journey, I am grateful that we arrived at Wukari mission without any major mishap. The bush road was a sea of mud with so much water on the surface I couldn't always see the edge of the road. We slithered, slipped, and bumped our way along using four-wheel drive, while the wiper blades struggled to keep my view clear from the flying debris and torrential rain. Twice I had to stop, once to remove tree limbs that had fallen across the path, the second time to put gas into the tank. Driving constantly in four-wheel-drive was burning up gas at an alarming rate.

Stepping out into this kind of storm in the dark, I suddenly realized just how valuable my houseboy Alfred was to me, and just how much he took care of things. It was a bad mistake deciding not to bring at least one of the boys along. Two jerry cans were racked on the front fender, as well as two on the rear. What I had never foreseen, however, was this sort of situation. All the cans were padlocked because of theft. There was one lock on the rack and another on each can, and when they were needed, it was normally Alfred who took charge. Now it was my turn, so I just stopped the truck under a huge cotton tree, hoping that it might give me some protection from the storm. Jack looked as if he was dozing. Neither of us had said one word since we left Igbudu.

"Jack," I said, leaning over so he could hear me, my mouth still partly numb, "I need to put some gas in the tank."

His eyes opened, and he partially removed the sterile pad he had been holding to his mouth. His slurred words were indistinct, but what I thought I heard him say was, "Try and make it quick."

By the light of my headlights, I fumbled with the locks, first on the racks and cans and then again on the fuel cap itself. I had to go back to the cab and reach under the seat for my emergency kit where I knew I had a small flashlight. The whole procedure was a mess and very painful. Holding the tiny flashlight in my swollen mouth, I struggled to pour in the gas, some of it splashing onto my shorts. Because I was wearing no rain gear, I was thoroughly soaked, my feet and legs covered with mud. I smelled awful and I didn't feel well at all. In sheer exasperation, I only put in what gas I thought was sufficient to get us back to Wukari, and I finally just heaved the jerry can into the back of the truck.

My steaming clothes only made the situation worse inside the cab. The windows soon began to fog, and I had to drive with my quarter window fully open to create enough airflow. This also meant that the right leg of my shorts continued to get soaked.

Wukari mission didn't have a generator, and as I pulled into the darkened compound, my headlights picked up scurrying figures moving forward holding small bush lights. After stopping the truck directly in front of the verandah steps, we both decided to make a run for it.

"Welcome back, Fathers," Jerome, the cook, greeted us. He was standing there holding a kerosene lamp. "Let me light the other lamps in the rooms, and then I will bring you food."

"Hi Jerome," I murmured, hardly able to move my lips. "We are not hungry and will go directly to our rooms." I could see that Jack was sleeping on his feet, and I needed a shower and a dry change of clothes. "Please have the boys bring in our bags; then you can go for the night. We will see you early in the morning."

"Yes, sir, Fathers, thank you, Fathers, good night, Fathers" he said, and shuffled off to light the lamps.

"Are you okay, Jack?" I asked. He had walked into the dining room and was pulling out a chair.

"Mike," he mumbled, "I feel lousy, but it will pass. How about you?"

"The same," I replied, "and I need to get out of these filthy clothes. The smell of the gas on my shorts is killing me. Just give me five minutes, then we can plan our journey for tomorrow."

"Fine. I think I'll have a glass of water. We also have a bunch of medication to take tonight."

The rains were a real concern for us. We both knew that we were into a real monsoon and while it seemed to be easing off now, we knew that it would start up again with a vengeance in the morning. My Land Rover was up to the task and would get us through to Abwa so Jack could pick up his own truck, but the roads would be so bad that I'd only be able to drive fairly slowly. It could take us all day.

"How are you feeling, Jack?" I asked the following morning as he walked into the dining room and headed for the refrigerator. He looked fresh after his shower, but his eyes looked very tired and his jaws still looked very swollen. "How is the mouth?"

"I'm extremely sore, but I'm not bleeding any more, and my mouth feels like the bottom of a parrot cage. I need a glass of water just now. But at least I no longer have a headache. I couldn't tell you just how bad my head felt on the road home last night. And how are you?" He sat down opposite me, slowly half-filling a glass as if he was not really sure he wanted it.

"About the same as you; I didn't sleep long enough," I said, pouring myself a coffee. "There were mosquitoes all over the place including one inside my net. I eventually found it, but then had difficulty getting back to sleep, so I've been up since six. I got the Voice of America news. The reception for BBC was just too poor. That Watergate scandal seems to be quite a thing over there. I wish I knew more about it. And it seems that the last US soldier has finally left Viet Nam. Would you please pass me the water?"

"Sure. Once I have a smoke and manage a cup of cool coffee, I might feel a bit better."

Our arrival at the ferry on the Katsinala River came as a relief. Even though we were just sitting there, it was a welcome respite from driving in the horrible weather and road conditions. The rain had started to ease off and we were on the river bank, surrounded by all kinds of vehicles. The swollen brown river was full of dangerous, floating debris. The water looked as if it had risen four or five feet since our crossing forty eight hours ago. Down at the water's edge, small groups of men could be seen and heard, milling around, shouting, gesticulating at each other, and pulling on ropes attached to a barge. It all looked very disorganized.

A young man, wearing a battered nondescript peaked cap, white plastic sunglasses, and an orange-colored hooded poncho with "I got rained on at Paul Masson Winery" on the back, clearly had some authority. He worked his way through the vehicles, stopping at the small trucks, then signaling occasionally for one to move forward.

"I am the Ferry Master," he announced pompously, peering through my half-open window like a hawk assessing its prey. It was instinctive, but I just knew he was on the prowl, looking for a "dash." "We are having problems keeping the barge moored, so we are only taking a few small vehicles over at a time and no big trucks at all." He paused to allow us time to digest this very important information.

But as if we were thinking in stereo, Jack leaned past me and said, "I know the barge captain. He is a friend of mine and I need to speak with him."

There was that Nigerian instant recognition of senior rank and its obligatory, unquestioning acceptance.

"Then take your place in that line over there immediately," he responded officiously, pointing to a much shorter line of vehicles. He was already moving away in search of more gullible victims, as he arrogantly dismissed us with a wave of his arm in the general direction of the ferry.

"It's our lucky day," I joked with Jack once we were on the barge. "Your ruse worked."

"Don't count on it," he quipped back, with just the beginnings of a smile, "this sucker might hit a log before we reach the other bank. We might be spending a night on some godforsaken island down river."

Fortunately, the crossing ended uneventfully.

"It will be good to get to Abwa," Jack said once we were on the road again. He was now in the driver's seat, having offered to take the wheel for this last leg of the journey. "Perhaps we should stay the night with Bob.

It will be dark in a couple of hours, and we both need a good night's rest. There's no point in pushing ourselves."

"That's a great idea," I responded. "If you can stay away from the college for another day, I certainly can delay going home."

It was strange seeing Bob standing in the driveway, holding an umbrella, waiting for us even before Jack had switched off the motor. There was always a general air of nervousness about him, evidenced by his constant non-stop chatter that was only interrupted as he paused to light one cigarette from another. In the grey evening light, his face seemed a little strained. This big gentle giant had a wonderful sense of humor, and throughout his twenty plus years in Nigeria, he had acquired the reputation of being a wonderful raconteur. He was also a great missionary. He came from a farming family, and his appointment to this agricultural school suited him perfectly.

"Oh my God," he exclaimed, opening the door on the driver's side, "am I glad to see you two. How are you both? Did you get your teeth fixed?" And before either of us could reply, he blurted out, "Brother Luke is dead."

"What?" we both cried in amazement.

"Yes, and the body is still here. Come inside quickly, and I'll tell you all about it."

"When did he die?" Jack asked, once we were seated in the living room.

"That's the problem, I really don't know. I went to Gboko on business just after you two left on Thursday, and only returned a few hours ago. Cook says Luke wasn't feeling well and went for a siesta. He did get up for dinner, but not for breakfast yesterday. I guess we can say he has been dead…" — he paused to check his wristwatch — "at least twenty-four hours, but it could be longer."

"Holy shit, Bob," I cried, "and in this heat!"

"Mother of God!" yelled Jack. "He needs to be buried immediately!"

"Well, I've dressed him in his monk's robe, and my carpenter is making a coffin as we speak."

"Why don't we take a look at the body and pay our respects?" I suggested. "He certainly merits a prayer from us."

We stood around the bed in silence, each one of us locked in our own thoughts, looking at this huge wax-like figure. Luke weighed almost three hundred pounds, even though he was only five feet seven inches tall. I had never seen him in his white, voluminous Franciscan robe before, and it somehow made him look even larger.

"Luke always said he wanted to be buried with his community," Bob announced, as were walking back to the sitting room, "and I feel obliged to take him to Adoka."

"But that's over a hundred miles from here," I interjected.

"What I need right now is a beer and some time to think," said Jack, heading off to the refrigerator. "Anyone else interested?"

"Sure, why not," Bob and I chorused.

"We need to think this through carefully," Jack said, handing over a bottle to each of us. "You are the senior person here, Bob, and Luke was also a member of your community, so what is your call?"

Bob was sitting on the edge of his easy chair, beer bottle in one hand, cigarette in the other, but he did not appear to be enjoying either. Unexpectedly, he suddenly put both down, ran a hand nervously through his thinning, gray hair and declared with almost pontifical solemnity, "I need to take his body to Adoka. It was Luke's last wish."

"But Bob," I argued, standing up to stretch my legs, "you know what the roads are like. You will have almost eighty miles of just mud before you reach the highway. Is this prudent? Both Jack and I are feeling like shit, and need to rest."

As if to underline my opinion, there was a brilliant flash of lightning that lit up the whole compound, followed almost immediately by a deafening clap of thunder that told us a storm was breaking right overhead. All of us jumped to our feet and rushed to close the shutters that we had opened earlier to help the room cool down. The torrential rain, driven by the wind, was already pouring into the house.

"Mike, I must do this," he insisted, as we stood huddled together in the middle of the floor.

"Well, if that's the decision, I move that we all travel together," suggested Jack. "And in addition, I also suggest, that we use Mike's Land Rover since none of our trucks has four-wheel drive." Addressing me directly, he asked, "Are you all right with that?"

"I'm fine," I replied, but inwardly I did not want to go. I was extremely tired and I suspected that Jack felt the same. This was an honorable, but an absolutely foolhardy journey to undertake.

"Then I need to get some gas from you Bob, if you don't mind." He was walking towards the back door but stopped and turned as I addressed him, "I'm into my reserves. If your mechanic is available, would you have him also check my oil and window washers? Here are my keys," I said, tossing them to him.

He caught them one handed, like a professional shortstop. "Not a problem, Mike, I can still see the lights over in the workshop. I'll talk to him right away. And while I'm there, I'll check on how my carpenter is doing with the coffin." Then, retrieving a tattered blue raincoat hanging on the wall, he managed to squeeze his huge, contorted frame into it. It was a couple of sizes too small, but he didn't seem to care, as he bent down his head and shoulders and sloshed his way into the dark storm.

Five minutes later he arrived back, this time with his carpenter and two assistants.

"Thank God," I whispered to Jack, "I don't wish to appear disrespectful, but the sooner we get this over with, the better. How much longer can the body hold out?"

"I'd rather not discuss it right now," he replied, "but it is a serious issue. We need to move quickly."

We all walked solemnly towards the small bedroom, led by Bob, the carpenter and his assistant carrying the coffin, and another man carrying the cover. "I will handle the body together with my staff," Bob announced, moving to the head of the bed. "We will place the coffin at the side of the bed, lift Luke up on his sheet, and then swing him over and into the coffin. The carpenter will then seal it."

The coffin itself was a very simple affair, made out of local, general purpose, white softwood. There were no decorations of any kind; no handles or fittings. It was made in the normal fashion we were all accustomed in this part of Nigeria: a simple, long rectangular box. As quietly and as reverently as he could, Bob began to organize the proceedings.

The carpenter and his assistant were instructed to each take hold of a corner of the sheet at the foot of the bed. Bob and the junior assistant held the sheet near Luke's cowled head.

"On the count of three, we will all lift together, and swing the body over the coffin," he whispered, as if he was trying not to wake up Luke.

"One, two, three. Oh, my God. Stop! For Christ's sake!" yelled Bob, the veins in his arms bulging, as he hung on to the sheet while the body hovered over the coffin, "He won't fit in, he won't fit in, it's too narrow."

I couldn't believe my ears, and was not in a position to see clearly, but I took Bob's word for it.

"Oh, my God, holy shit!" he exclaimed. "What a mess!" They then somehow managed to heave the body back onto the bed. Quickly taking charge again, Bob whispered something to the carpenter. Reaching into the back pocket of his dark brown coveralls, he carefully retrieved a steel tape, extended it, laid it across Luke's shoulders, and then checked the measurement with the coffin. Unhurriedly and methodically, he repeated the exercise two more times. There was a look of disbelief and utter confusion on his face, as he meticulously jotted down his findings with a stubby pencil in what looked like a child's notebook. Then, sticking the end of the pencil into his mouth, he wet it and painstakingly checked and re-checked his calculations. It was clear that Bob was correct, and had just saved everybody some embarrassment. The team slowly gathered up their materials, and left in a silent solemn procession.

The three of us regrouped in the dining room.

"Well, what's next?" I asked, dragging out a chair and flopping on to it.

"It will probably take them the best part of an hour to fix everything," Bob mumbled, lighting up yet another cigarette and offering the packet to Jack who also lit one up. With all the windows in the house being closed, the smoke began to affect my eyes. I tried opening a louver, but the rain was still being driven into the side of the house.

"So, what about something to eat? Can you guys manage some soup and mashed yams? I know my cook is preparing it."

Jack and I looked at each other, and then decided we needed some nourishment and should try to eat something. We both nodded in agreement.

The second attempt with the coffin was much better. Everything went as planned. I backed the Land Rover up to the front steps, lowered my tailgate and watched from the shelter of the verandah, as they placed the coffin in the truck, all the employees getting thoroughly soaked as the rain sheeted off the gutterless metal roof. Our bags were thrown in next to it, as well as an extra six-foot-long plank I had asked for, as a precaution in case we got completely bogged down on the road.

"There is one small issue we should talk about before we leave," I announced, as we stood on the verandah waiting for the canvas covers on the truck to be secured. "My truck only has two real seats. There is a small seat in the middle, but it is tiny. Both of you guys are big, so what's the solution, as I'm sure no one wants to ride in the back?"

"Well, how about this," suggested Bob, "if you don't mind, Mike, I'll drive since I know the road better than both of you, and we can squeeze you in between us."

It seemed pointless to discuss it further. "Okay, let's give it a try," I responded half-heartedly.

It was cramped, uncomfortable and extremely hot inside the cab. Outside the rain and wind had turned the roads into a sea of red mud as the truck bounced, bucked, and slithered its way into the night. It took quite some time for Bob to get used to the long stick shift, the super heavy clutch, and the weight of the truck itself. Twice we stopped to negotiate streams that had appeared across the road, and the only way to check them for depth was to get out and wade across. These were welcome breaks for me, but they also meant that both Jack and I got soaked. An hour into the journey, it almost came to an end. We came upon about twenty vehicles, all stopped. Most of the drivers and passengers had rigged up tarps between the trees in the jungle alongside the road and had created makeshift shelters. They were chatting and cooking on open fires. It was clear that they had been there for some time.

"What's the problem?" Bob shouted out of his window to one of the people sitting near a fire.

"A tanker has jack-knifed and blocked the road. They have sent word to the Public Works Department in Yandev to bring a bulldozer so it can be towed. It will be here in the morning."

If this was true, it did not sound like good news at all. "Let's head up there," Bob said, "and take a look for ourselves."

Sure enough, the tanker was right across the road, its rear wheels almost up to the axles in water and mud. There was no way it could be moved. In the light of the nearest truck's headlights, two filthy almost-naked men were futilely digging a huge hole, trying to get some planks under its wheels. The only good news for these workers was that the rain was easing off and the wind was dying down.

Off to the right hand side of the tanker, another group of men was swinging machetes, trying to clear a path much closer to the jungle that would allow them to possibly drive around the tanker. We all exited the cab to get a close look.

"Should I try to take us through?" asked Bob.

"Absolutely not," I replied testily "you have no idea of the ground. It might look fine, but once you put the truck on to it, God alone knows what might happen. I suggest that we turn around, which would be difficult in itself, and head back to Abwa."

"But Mike, I really have to try. The clock is ticking against us."

"I know that, Bob," I snapped, walking back to my truck. "Jack, what do you say? Do we go for it or not?"

"Well, we're here, Mike, we may as well go for broke. If it doesn't work, we should turn back immediately."

In hindsight, I was stupid for letting Bob get behind the wheel. I had sensed all along that he was quite unfamiliar with such a heavy truck, and especially with using four-wheel drive. Squeezing his way alongside the stranded wagons, he finally caught up with us at the new detour. I had arranged to give him a signal before he entered it, since I wanted to walk every inch of it first. I can only assume he forgot the arrangement, for I had no sooner started to wade through the almost knee-deep mud when he accelerated and tried to charge through it. He almost made it past the tanker, but suddenly came to an abrupt stop. All four wheels started spinning madly and digging themselves into deep holes.

"Stop, Bob, for Christ's sake, stop!!" I yelled at the top of my voice. "You'll burn out the clutch."

We were well and truly bogged down. "We need the plank," I said. "Let's try and get it under the front wheels, and I'll see if they will pull us out."

Jack undid the straps of the canvas cover and climbed into the back. "I can't get hold of it," he said, "I can't see what I'm doing. Could you pass me the flashlight, Mike?"

"Sure, not a problem," I answered, reaching into my emergency kit and passing the light to him through the cab's rear sliding window.

"Oh, my God," he announced. "The coffin has split, and there is a terrible smell in here. I guess all that bouncing around was too much for it."

I immediately closed the window, jumped out of the cab, and helped him remove the plank.

We tried for about ten minutes to place it right under the wheels, but each time the truck slipped off.

"Bob, Jack, let's talk," I said, leaning against the front fender so I could rest a little. "Look at us. We are all filthy, wet, and tired. The road in front of us, even if we could pass, will not be better than this, and we need to do something about the coffin." Bob lit up another cigarette, the lighted match blinding me momentarily. In the dark, I could not see Jack's face, as he too leaned against the truck, but I sensed that he was bone tired, as he had spoken very little since we left Abwa.

"We need to head back to Abwa. Do we agree?"

They both concurred.

"We have one last chance to get out of this, or we could be stuck here for hours, possibly a whole day, and I would hate to think what we will have to do with Luke's body then. It will take some coordination and lots of luck, but I will try and winch us around so that we are least facing in the right direction." Prior to shipping this particular Land Rover from the UK, I'd had it fitted with several upgrades, including an additional set of headlights, an extra large fuel tank, and a front-end power winch. I had never had to use it previously, so I was unsure as to its performance.

"Bob, I want you to take this," I said handing him the cable which had a large hook attached to it, "and wrap it around a tree on the opposite side of the road, at almost forty five degrees from where we are."

"Just hang on for a second," he urged; "let me get my big flashlight from my bag." He vanished for a few seconds as he clambered over the tailgate, and a couple of quick flashes indicated that he had found it and it was in working order. I'm not sure of what exactly happened next or how it occurred, but as he was throwing one leg out of the truck, his other muddy foot slipped, and he almost fell out on his face. He was saved by the leg of his wide, old fashioned shorts getting caught on the corner of the jerry can rack, and for a couple of moments, he was fully suspended in mid air.

"Holy shit!" he yelled. "What the fuck is happening?" His flashlight landed in the mud followed immediately by the sound of ripping fabric. Then he too landed in it face down

"Are you all right?" Jack shouted with concern, hearing his unusual expletives, and quickly moving to the rear of the truck. Seeing Bob on all fours he asked, "What happened?" helping him to his feet.

"I'm okay," said Bob, "but I dropped my flashlight. It's around here somewhere." Fumbling in his pocket he quickly produced and lit a match, shielding it from the breeze with his cupped hands. "There it is," he said gratefully, reaching down for it as the match died. Then coming back to the cab, he wiped off some of the mud from the glass with his now filthy shirt saying, "I hope the damn thing still works."

"Then grab the cable again, Bob, and run it out to that big tree over there." I stuck my arm out of the window, pointing into the jungle. The outline of trees was clearly visible in the side glow of the powerful head-lights. Jack was leaning on my door as I released the winch clutch, and Bob began pulling out the cable.

"Oh, my God!" he shouted laughingly at Bob, "Look at yourself. You are almost showing your ass!"

I had been focusing on the engine control panel, and at first failed to notice the state of Bob's clothing. In addition to being covered in mud, one leg of his shorts was now torn right up to his belt, and he was showing a very white thigh and underwear. I couldn't control myself and burst out laughing. Jack guffawed for the first time that night. It seemed that this solemn occasion was fast turning into a circus. But it was a very funny sight. Jack and I were in hysterics, and in spite of our still sore mouths couldn't stop laughing. Bob's nonchalance made it even funnier. A small crowd of onlookers had gathered, hearing the motor start and seeing the headlights come on.

We all held our breath, as I engaged the clutch and let the winch take up the slack in the cable. Slowly it tightened and ever so carefully, I added more power until the truck gave a little jerk; then the front end, thank-fully, began to move. I was surprised that it was so easy. We were quickly broadside across the road, in front of the tanker.

"Let's do it again," I urged pointing to another tree further down to our left. This time it was Jack who offered to help, dragging and setting up the cable. Bob stood outside the cab door smoking, seemingly unfazed with what had happened.

Repeating the procedure two more times, we finally ended up facing back the way we had come, and were now on the crown of the road.

"If we can all squeeze up tight, I'll take us back," I announced, after we had put the plank away and I'd rewound the cable. "We're not out of this mess yet, but I know this truck's capability best." There was no argument, but once we were all inside, even with the windows open, it was extremely hot and humid, and there was a distinct odor coming into the cab from the rear of the truck. We all knew what we had to do, and time was against us.

Back at Abwa, we stood together for a few minutes in the driveway, waiting for the generator to fire up. Bob's boys were there in various stages of undress, no doubt wondering what had brought us back so soon.

"One of you remove the bags from the truck, and put them into the guest rooms," Bob said. "Also I need one of our small tarps, about ten feet square, and some thin ropes brought to Father's truck right away. Tell Okeke and the carpenter to come here immediately."

They quickly scurried off into the night, clearly sensing the urgency in Bob's voice.

"Let's take a quick shower, and change into some clean clothing," he suggested as we walked into the house.

"You two know where the visitors' rooms are. I will have the cook make us some coffee, and I'll arrange for my mechanic to take the back hoe and dig a grave at the side of the orchard. It shouldn't take him too long, perhaps thirty or forty minutes. My staff will put the coffin on a push cart once we have made it secure, and bring it over when the grave is ready."

A little after two a.m. we conducted a sad and unusual, and yet in a weird sort of way, very reverent ceremony. The rains had stopped, and the wind died down somewhat. The intermittent light from the watery moon as it danced between the scudding, black clouds cast a sepulchral glow over the orchard. Bob, Jack and I and three of Bob's staff lowered the coffin, now securely wrapped in a bright blue tarp, into the ground.

We all stood silently, as Bob, with the aid of a flashlight, read some final prayers. The loneliness of the setting, of death itself, suddenly hit me. Here was a man, an educator who had dedicated his whole life to teaching others. Literally thousands of people must have known him in his lifetime on three continents, yet his body was being buried in the middle of the night, with only the spotlights from a back-hoe for guidance. He was being laid to rest in a remote part of Africa, away from his own family and his religious community, with just a small group of brothers paying their last respects.

CHAPTER 11

Betrayal

*T*HUMP… THUMP…I lay there waiting, knowing what was coming next. THUMP...THUMP. My co-pastor, Andy, had taken his shower and was performing his early morning rituals, and I knew that at this very minute he was putting his socks on. Through my bedroom wall, I could hear his muffled voice. He constantly talked to himself.

In exactly four minutes, his door would slam. With Andy doors were never gently closed. They were treated like obstacles in his path. He always walked on his heels, with a brisk, purposeful military stride, as if heading off to some important meeting. A sense of great urgency exuded from this man. With head down, shoulders hunched, his shoes clattering on the bare cement floor, he would soon head off down the long hallway towards the church. The outside door would slam. It would be six-twenty-five precisely, and Andy would soon be in the church, ready to celebrate the six-thirty mass. I could have set my watch by his movements.

He was considerably older than me, but only ordained five years before me, having entered the seminary after spending twenty years as a professional soldier in the British army. A good deal of that time was spent in the Middle East, primarily Cyprus and Aden. He still exhibited signs of his basic preparation for those assignments. We had only been together for a week or so, when I became intrigued by these mysterious early morning thumping sounds, so I asked him if he knew the source. With a genuine look on his face, of complete bewilderment, he responded, "And you don't do it, Father Michael?" he responded quizzically. Unlike the rest of my colleagues and friends, he always gave people their full title and name, and never used diminutives.

"Do what, Andy?"

"Make sure that that there are no scorpions in your shoes. They are very crafty creatures and like dark places."

"Aha," I thought. "And after all these years have you ever actually discovered one in a shoe?" I asked, half teasingly.

"No, but I never want to either. You never know, you just never know."

I guess he was just that kind of person: always serious, somewhat anxious, and hyper-vigilant. His powers of observation were also somewhat limited. Otherwise he would have noticed that I never wore shoes, only sandals!

After spending the last three years alone in Jato Aka, I had requested a move to a community setting. I craved companionship. Frankly, I was not only tired of living on my own, I had made a decision that I would never live that way again. Of the nine years I had spent in Nigeria, the last seven of them had been in one-man parishes. The loneliness and solitude had left their mark. With no phones, no radios, no TV, no newspapers, and mail perhaps every six weeks, it was easy to feel isolated. Since I lived fifty-five miles across the bush from my nearest neighbor, visits were few, brief, and sporadic. I had seen what this had done to other priests over time, and I was shocked at what was beginning to happen to me. It's easy to become self-centered, insensitive, and controlling when there is no one there to give you feedback or voice a contrary opinion. I welcomed my transfer to Adikpo.

The mission was one of the largest in the diocese, and there was much more work than could be handled by two priests. The mission compound itself was huge, covering about ten acres, and was organized in the form of a square. It contained not only a modern parish house and church, but a convent, and a large and very busy maternity and general clinic operated by Holy Rosary Sisters. Happily for me, my friend Terry Shields was one of them.

There was a grade school, and a high school, with more than a thousand students in total. At the far end near the market was a most recent development. A group of native nuns, Ibos, had moved into the old convent. They were teachers and were working in makeshift classrooms while the new girls' college was still under construction. Les Turner, the priest in charge of the project, was temporarily living with Andy and me.

Several weeks after I arrived, another priest was assigned to us, Nigel Morgan. He had been the pastor of a parish on the other side of the diocese, and I was surprised at his sudden arrival. Rumors about this man had circulated for a long time. They had even reached me when I was living a hundred and fifty miles away in Udei.

"What's the deal with Nigel?" I asked Andy one morning, as we worked in the office trying to coordinate our calendars for our safaris. I raised my voice slightly since Andy had what he called a "bad ear." Actually he was stone deaf in one ear, the result of an accident when he was in the army. "I know the Bishop must have spoken to you about him."

"Well, Father Michael, I can't say too much. But yes, you are correct. I was asked if he could come to Adikpo. We need another pair of hands, and Nigel had to move in a hurry."

"What do you mean, in a hurry?" I asked, stopping what I was writing and staring over at him.

"There was an issue with a local woman, and that's all I can tell you. The Bishop asked me not to discuss the details."

This sort of secrecy just ticks me off as being completely unnecessary and infantilizing. I am tired of things being swept under the rug. I just wish that the Bishop and his advisors would be honest with all of us. What are they afraid of?

"Okay, Andy," I responded, standing up and stretching. Even though it was early morning and the house had been built so that the office would not catch the full sun, it was already very warm inside. "But I am so tired of this diocese not dealing with its personnel issues. You and I know that rumors have been flying around for years about Nigel and his women. It's no secret that he rarely stays in a parish more than a year. Why do they move him around? Why don't the authorities take some definitive action?" I leaned against the open breeze block wall; it was nice and cool to the touch.

"I cannot tell you more. However, I would ask you to just keep your eyes and ears open and should you ever hear of anything negative concerning him, you must let me know right away."

"Fine," I replied. I knew Andy well enough to know that the subject was closed for now.

Some weeks later, Nigel and I were together checking on the progress at a new fifty-bed hospital we were building on the other side of town. He was both gregarious and gifted: he played the guitar and sang, was an extraordinary painter both in oils and watercolor, and also a certified architect. He loved to cook and took great pleasure in preparing unusually refined dishes for us, in stark contrast to the very simple native food that I was more accustomed to. Eager to learn as much as I could from him, I'd asked if I could accompany him. "Of course, Mike, it would be a pleasure."

A tall blond haired well-built forty-five year old, he moved with the easy suppleness of an athlete, and even in this sweaty heat, looked fresh and cool, as if ready to step onto a movie set. He exuded competence, composure, and a professional savoir-faire. He was also very apostolic and committed to his ministry. I was envious of his fluency in Tiv. Unlike me who had lived in three completely different linguistic regions, he had spent all of his time working with just the Tiv tribe. His command of the language was such that, to great acclaim from several linguists, he had just written a native prayer book.

It was so easy to talk with this man, and we struck up a mutually comfortable relationship, even though we had only met twice, very briefly and casually, prior to his recent assignment. Still, it came as a complete surprise when he confided in me.

We were walking side by side back to the truck when he suddenly stopped next to a makeshift carpenter's bench under the shade of a huge mango tree. There was nobody working; it was siesta time and they had all finished for the day. With one hand, he casually took out a packet of cigarettes from the top pocket of his safari shirt, flicked open the lid with his thumb, and shook a cigarette expertly between his lips. With his other hand, he deftly flipped open his Zippo lighter.

"Oh, I'm sorry," he said remorsefully, offering me the packet. "Please forgive my bad manners." And then, he caught himself. "Ah, but you don't smoke, do you?"

"I used to," I said, "but I quit some years ago after a bad bout of malaria followed by a dose of pneumonia. But don't worry about it." My sixth sense told me that he was about to say something I should pay attention to.

He took a long satisfying pull, and then let the smoke gently drift upwards in one long exhale. Placing his bush hat on the bench, he shook his fairly long and now flattened hair loose, running his fingers through it.

"I suppose you are no different from anyone else in the diocese, and are wondering why I was transferred to Adikpo," he mused out loud.

"Well, I must admit, it had crossed my mind," I responded, wondering where all of this was going, "and you know how the grapevine and rumor mill is in this diocese."

"Well, let me give it you straight from the horse's mouth, so to speak: I was having an affair with a Tiv woman. It had been going on for about seven months." And before I could respond, as if anticipating questions he quickly continued, "she was not married, but actually a widow; her husband was killed some time ago in an auto accident. She had no kids and was a trained teacher. I tried to be very discreet."

I leaned back against the workbench, as if to gather my thoughts; I was not sure just how I should respond.

"What do you want me to say, Nigel? You know I cannot condone your behavior, or is this you wanting to make your confession?"

"Oh! No. I have already been to confession," he quickly responded.

"Then let me ask you this," I replied. "Are the rumors true that you have been involved with several women?"

This time there was no pause, no hesitation. It was as if he'd been waiting for the flood gates to be released. He turned towards me, and staring into my eyes with real earnestness, he said, "Let's walk under the trees, Mike, it will be a little cooler, and I'll give you the whole story."

Yes, Nigel had had multiple sexual relationships, and each time they had been discovered. After one particularly scandalous and notorious occurrence, the Bishop had sent him back to the UK in order for the furor to die down. Eighteen months later he was back in Nigeria where he continued to get sexually involved. Once these relationships came to light, for the most part the authorities simply wanted to put a lid on the fallout, and would transfer Nigel to another parish. In two similar cases involving other priests, the diocese paid college tuition for some of the women's children in order to hush up the affairs.

In the space of one hour, I learned more than I really wanted to about the graphic details of this priest's conflicted past: the loneliness, the solitude, the lying, the duplicity, the misuse of mission funds, the loving and the being loved, the first adolescent approaches to sex, the separations and the breakups. His was a tortured soul, and though I could not excuse his behavior, I at least began to understand it and feel some compassion for him.

"But Nigel," I asked, once we were back in the truck, "I am curious. You were taking an immense risk; did you never get any of these women pregnant?"

"Not that I know of," he replied, "at least none of them has ever claimed that I am the father of their children." He said this with almost an element of regret in his voice.

"And how many of your affairs involved native women?" I inquired.

There was a pause. I was driving and working my way around a broken culvert which meant navigating down the steep bank of a dried up stream and up the other side, all the while avoiding some nasty rocks. I also could not delay. I needed to get back to the mission as I had a scheduled Bible study class later that evening.

It came out in a staccato, benumbed, emotionless sort of way. "All of them," he said, "all of them."

There were so many more questions I wanted to ask. "Wouldn't it have been safer with a nun or one of the expatriate teachers? What would you have done if there had been a pregnancy? Etc."

"I can understand your loneliness, Nigel," I replied, "and your need to be loved, but why don't you just leave the priesthood, find the right woman, and settle down and have a family? Why put yourself and these women through this? Apart from everything else, the emotional strain must be unbearable."

"It's really out of the question, Mike," he responded somewhat pensively. "My mother is still alive, and if I left the priesthood it would kill her. And don't forget, my family's Catholic heritage goes back centuries. We are so well known in England. I have three uncles who are priests, one a Spiritan, one a Monsignor, another a Benedictine monk. Even if I could bring myself to make a decision to leave, which I cannot, it would cause such a huge scandal I would probably never be able to get a job in the UK."

I felt that this was a bit of an exaggeration. And in any case, there were other options such as going to the USA or France. After all, he knew that other priests had left the priesthood and survived.

I would have liked to continue the sharing, but as we drove into the mission I could see a line of people already heading towards the church and my Bible class. I needed to take a quick shower and change into some clean clothes. We would talk more later.

Dinner that night was notable only because of what happened between Nigel and Les Turner. Les was really only lodging with us until the college buildings were completed; meanwhile, he paid us rent for his room and board. Since I was in charge of the money, I was also responsible for the purchase of food, and for paying the salaries of the cook and houseboys. Les, however, had a terribly suspicious mind and believed that he was paying too much for his lodging.

No sooner had Stephen, our cook, presented the food on the table when Les helped himself to a very large portion. Almost before Nigel and I had been served, Les, who had wolfed down his food, was already looking for a second helping. Andy, however, was late, so Nigel suggested that we set aside a plate for him first.

"There is no need," replied Les sarcastically. "If Andy truly cared about the community, he would be here on time,"

"He's up at the maternity clinic," said Nigel, taking hold of a plate and preparing to measure out a portion. "He probably had an emergency. Andy is so reliable and organized he would not keep us waiting without reason. I'll send his food to the kitchen, so that the cook can keep it warm."

"Absolutely not," said, Les, his voice clearly rising in irritation. "If he is late, he can get what is left. Meanwhile, Nigel, I would appreciate it if you would give me a second serving; after all I am paying more than anyone in this house for the food."

"I am sorry, Les," replied Nigel, maintaining his composure at this stupidity and bad manners, "but I am keeping a plate for Andy." And with that he fixed the portion and handed it over to our houseboy William to take to the kitchen.

"Then I will take everything that remains," cried Les, by this time almost in tears. Standing up, he reached over for the serving dish, his large horn-rimmed glasses making his bulging, panda-like eyes look like they were about to pop out of his head.

I could not believe that such stupidity and childishness could come out of the mouth of a priest. It began to dawn on me that Les was not just obsessive, he was really mentally quite sick.

"Les, there is no need to get worked up about this," said Nigel gently. "It's only food, and there is more in the refrigerator if you need it." But it was the wrong thing to say, at the wrong time, to the wrong person.

Les was highly educated, with a master's degree in administration, in addition to his degrees in philosophy and theology. He had held a government position and was capable of building and operating a large college, and had actually spent a brief time in a bush parish. But where was he emotionally I pondered? When I first arrived in Adikpo, I was awakened by him one night, flashlight in hand as he tip-toed past my room heading for the dining room. I presumed he was going for a bottle of cold water. But each night it was the same, and I failed to understand why he wouldn't take a bottle of water to his room, when he retired for the night rather than having to get up. So on one of his nightly forays, I followed him. There he was taking the food items out of the refrigerator, checking them, counting them onto the kitchen table, and then replacing them. It was surreal. How could a grown, educated mature priest be so obsessed with food?

"What do you mean, only food?" screamed Les, "I have paid for it. It's people like you," he yelled, pointing a finger at Nigel, "that do not care that this cook is a thief, and is feeding his whole family at my expense. And this new houseboy that you brought into the mission is just as bad. You, you have no regard for anybody. Look at your own behavior. You are a disgrace to the priesthood." He paused for a moment to clean his glasses which were steamed over.

"Les, please," I interjected, "that last comment is totally uncalled for. If nothing else, it is unchristian. If you have issues with the food, then please address them to me. Nigel was absolutely correct to do what he did for Andy."

At this point he was unable to contain himself. "Don't you talk to me about being unchristian? You are as bad as he is," he screeched, pointing at Nigel, then turning to me, "Your scandalous affair with Sister Terry is the talk of the diocese."

My mouth dropped open, eyes bulging as I stood with my fingertips pressing into the table. I leaned forward like a bull about to charge.

"What the hell are you talking about?" I stormed.

He ignored my angry shout. Spittle sprayed from his mouth as he continued to rant. "I will not sit and eat with either of you two hypocrites."

"Hypocrites?" I demanded. "You need help, Les. You're clearly delusional."

A line of drool now appeared on his chin, causing me to instinctively wipe my own mouth, as I contemplated Les going completely mad.

He tossed his head in the air and pushing his chair over, stormed out of the room.

I raised my hands, palms up, and looked at Nigel unable to speak.

He simply lowered his head, shaking it from side to side.

"Good Lord," I said, "what was that all about, and what is that crap about Sister Terry? Can't I have a nun for a friend without someone thinking that we are sleeping together?"

"Apparently not," Nigel said.

I sat down and stared straight ahead, just looking out into the darkness.

Nigel shook his head and frowned.

"It also looks like we are not going to have Les for a dinner companion any longer," he said, "at least not after that explosion. I expect that he'll eat with his new employees, the Ibo Sisters of Notre Dame."

The following morning, my prayer time was suddenly interrupted by a call for help.

"Father Mike, come quickly, come quickly!" It was our catechist, James, calling me through the office window. "Sister Terry needs you at the maternity clinic." The building was only about a hundred yards away, so grabbing my ministry bag, I ran over as fast as I could.

"Where is the Sister in charge?" I asked the midwife.

"She is in the outpatient emergency room, Father. They have brought in a young girl from Mbape with a head wound."

With no hospital nearby, this sort of thing happened all the time. A maternity clinic had to be prepared to handle all kinds of cases, even though there was no doctor available.

When I entered the room, a young fourteen-year-old girl was lying unconscious on the table. Sister Terry and a nurse were working on her, trying to stop the blood flow from what appeared to be a huge hole in the girl's forehead. It was only as I got close that I was shocked into recognition. This was Monica, and I had been at her school in Mbape just two days previously. We had spoken at length that day, and she had asked me, if I would petition the Sisters to give her an interview for a trainee position. A child as young as this, so vibrant, energetic and with so much potential should not be so close to death. But this was Africa.

"Mike, I need you to start praying," were the first words out of Terry's mouth. "She has a spear wound that has pierced her forehead and gone into the brain. I am afraid for her. There is not much I can do."

I prayed the Church's prayer for the sick and anointed her with holy oil. Then taking hold of her right hand, I prayed to the God I knew, without words, letting my heart speak for itself, simply willing Him to hold her in the palm of His hand, wanting Him to heal her. My heart was thumping as I struggled to contain the powerful emotions running through me.

"I'm losing her," said Terry softly. "Keep praying Mike. She is going into shock."

I briefly opened my eyes, and the telltale signs were there: rapid breathing, clammy moist skin, erratic pulse. I squeezed her hand, wanting to somehow transmit my life into her. I do not know long I stood there, but it must have been quite a while. I felt Terry gently separate my hand from Monica's whispering to me, "She has gone, Mike. She has gone."

When Terry had finished her shift that evening, I went over to the convent to visit with the sisters, which I usually did when I was not on safari. Later Terry and I spent time together, just the two of us in the tiny chapel, holding hands, praying silently in the dark for Monica. There I learned the full, tragic story. Two school kids were fooling around throwing a spear, and Monica unknowingly had walked directly into its flight.

When I first arrived in Adikpo, I had shared with Andy as much as I could about my relationship with Terry, and especially that she really was my spiritual confidante. Being the kind of person he was, he appreciated my openness, but struggled to understand how any woman, even a nun, could advise a priest on anything. We were together in the parish church looking at some remodeling I had started, and he responded in typical fashion. "Father Michael, I will not pretend to understand it. My training was very different from yours. But if it is helping you, I can live with it. Just keep it open and honest."

"Thanks Andy," I replied, "I too want everything to be open and above board. If you ever have an issue with it, then let me know, and we will take care of it together."

"Well, I do have an issue right now," he said. "I'm concerned as to how the other nuns in Sister Terry's community are handling your relationship."

"So why don't you go over and talk with them?" I urged. "Hear things for yourself."

Being a very simple and direct man in all his interactions, I knew he would deal with it head on. As fortune would have it, that opportunity came the next day. The Superior of the convent, Sister Maryann, had received information from the Bishop that a philanthropic group from Ireland wished to donate a considerable amount of money for development of the clinic. She invited Andy over for a preliminary discussion. He later told me that he had presented to her the issue of my relationship with Terry.

"I was very happy to hear that the community was unanimous in their positive acceptance of it," he reported. "Maryann had her doubts at first since she was unsure as to what it was all about, but she is totally at ease now."

As time went on, Andy tolerated Terry; I think that deep down he was afraid of her. She challenged his theology and questioned his understanding of the changes in religious life being called for by Rome. He was set in his ways and held a very traditional view of how nuns should act. He and I invited all of the sisters over to the mission once a week for dinner, and we usually had animated and fascinating discussions about our ministry, and the need to replace ourselves with native nuns and priests.

Nigel helped create a relaxed atmosphere with his guitar playing, and four of the nuns, being Irish, kept us entertained with songs. Andy was always nice and courteous with them, but I believe he was just too uncomfortable to really relax, seeing them without veils, voicing their own opinions about religion, enjoying a beer, and Terry usually smoking. These were liberated nuns, and Andy's old-school training made it difficult for him to cope with them.

At the beginning of the rainy season Terry went home to Philadelphia for three months. I remember it well; it was St Patrick's' Day. The heavens opened with a cloudburst, and she was sent off with best wishes for a safe journey to the airport four hundred miles away just as a monsoon hit the area.

Staff had come from the clinic, and a large group of women from neighboring villages, many of them with native food and small gifts, gathered in the rain in front of the convent steps and sang a couple of songs. They were a colorful bedraggled crowd, those with babies on their backs struggling to protect them with their umbrellas. The rest stood there stoically getting soaked.

Terry came out and spoke briefly to them in Tiv. I had been at the convent much earlier to celebrate mass for the sisters, had breakfast with the community, and said my good-bye. Even though she needed a much deserved rest, I knew I would really miss her.

The rains, driven by gale force winds came down so heavily that all Nigel and I could do was watch and wave from our verandah. And even then we got quite wet as the storm squalled and gusted erratically.

The group of native women, all of them barefooted trudged slowly towards the church through the many streams now running ankle-deep down the driveway. Seeking to obtain some minimal shelter under its eaves, they waited imperturbably in typical African fashion, to get a final glimpse of their friend. Then the small white and red ambulance came to collect her. Wearing a dark blue raincoat, with her head down and distinctive, long jet black-hair flying about uncontrollably, she looked over quickly in our direction, waved one last time, and was gone.

I missed not having her there to talk to. I missed her counsel and the opportunity to pray together. But in spite of the rains, I also had much to keep me occupied. I had a school that had lost part of its roof, and I was helping a small group of farmers in a remote corner of the parish, Udegi Beki, form a cooperative and micro credit union. We had done all of our surveys, formed a committee, taken monthly collections for the materials, and were now constructing a small rice mill. It was soon to be completed and before the end of the rains, I planned to obtain and install a diesel generator purchased with the help of my friends in the UK. Everything would be ready for harvest time. Preaching the Gospel was one thing, but for me this was the Gospel in action, and this was where my heart really was, helping people in a practical manner.

Returning home one evening after a long hard day in Udegi - we had had to dig the truck out of the mud several times - I was thrilled to find a letter from Terry waiting for me. Refreshed by a cool shower and a clean change of clothing, I relaxed before dinner in my bedroom-study, and quietly read news from the USA. It was a long letter filled with snippets and items that she knew would be of interest to me. She concluded her letter "yours affectionately," and also included a sticky note containing a well-known cartoon entitled "Love Is…." This one read, "Love is…Thinking About Each Other." I was touched by this gesture, showing that she genuinely cared about me, but I had already known that for a long time. Without any further thought, I stuck the note on my reading lamp, replaced the letter in its envelope, left it on my desk, and went out to join Nigel and Andy for dinner.

The following day the rains were torrential, and I had to cancel a trip I had planned to perform baptisms in a nearby village. Instead, I took the opportunity to visit our local school and spend some time with the teachers in charge of religious instruction. I must have looked a sorry sight as I arrived in the staff room, since my umbrella had blown inside out and I was soaked. I was wearing my sandals, and my legs were now covered with red mud whipped up by the strong winds, but nobody made any comment. I loved this about Nigeria. People accepted you as you were. Dennis Agabe, the headmaster, made me feel very welcome and insisted that I go to his house afterwards with some of his teachers and have a meal. It was a joyous occasion, filled with laughter, music, great banter and unaffected friendship. The Tiv people do not have the nickname "the Nigerian Irish" for nothing.

Les Turner was pacing up and down the long hallway, reading his prayer book, when I returned late that afternoon. He did not look well; his face was drawn and serious.

"Mike, I have something I need to discuss with you," was his opening greeting.

"Sure," I replied. "Just give me time to get out of these damp clothes and take a quick shower, and I will be right with you." I wondered what was on his mind; had he received bad news from home? His brother had been ailing and seriously sick for some time. Had he died?

He was seated at his desk as I entered his bedroom-study, and I flopped into an easy chair at the side of his desk.

"What is it Les?" I said breezily. "What can I do for you?"

"Mike, what I am about to say is not easy for me. I have prayed about it, and asked for God's guidance. I need to talk to you about your relationship with Sister Terry. I do not approve of it, and I believe that you are living in sin by prostituting your vocation and breaking the holy vow of celibacy." Not even once did he look at me, but kept staring down at the pencil in his hands, the whole time turning it over repeatedly from end to end. "As a brother priest, I am counseling you break it off once and for all."

I was so flabbergasted, words failed me. My comfortable, satisfying world in one blinding second had suddenly exploded. I was in a daze, a sort of fog. The ticking of the wall clock above Les's desk sounded exceedingly loud, and I was mesmerized by a struggling, beautiful orange and black moth, caught up in a large spider's web high up in the corner of the room. Thoughts and words refused to fully formulate, as they were swimming around in my head in some sort of molasses-like goo. I was just about to answer, when Les, holding up his hand as if to prevent my response, continued.

"You do not need to try and defend yourself." He was staring over my right shoulder as if addressing somebody else. "While you were out, I was searching for a book in your room, and I noticed this love note stuck to your desk light. I was both shocked and alarmed, as it confirmed my deepest concerns. Then I could not help noticing the letter you had left on your desk with a US stamp, sent by Sister Terry, and I felt obliged to read it. It is painfully obvious from its tone that the two of you are having an affair, and I am concerned that there will be a terrible scandal in this parish."

I had heard enough. Rising quickly from my seat, and looking him directly in the face, I struggled to control the gamut of emotions I was experiencing. "This is not brotherly love," I scoffed. "This is character assassination. You dared to read my mail, rummage through my things. You are a total asshole."

"Mike, that is a most unkind thing to say…"

"Just shut up and listen, Les," I snapped back, my anger now getting the better of me. "You are an uncharitable, intrusive, evil-minded bastard. I suggest that you finish building your house as soon as possible, and live where it will be safe for everybody — on your own."

The chair flew sideways, as I quickly turned and tripped over it in my haste to exit. I needed to think. I needed some fresh air. Les just continued sitting there as if pole-axed, starring into that same vacant space.

Later that evening, once Les had gone to his evening meal at the convent, I shared the incident with Andy and Nigel, explaining what had transpired. Both expressed surprise and shock that he would read my mail. Strangely, neither passed any comment on the "Love Is…" note. Andy, however, did tell Nigel that he had been made aware of the relationship all along and was reconciled to it. He also said that he would have a talk with Les later that night.

It was almost two weeks later that we had a surprise visitor; it was one of my closest friends, Jack Groves, who had recently been elected as the Regional Superior of the Spiritans in Makurdi Diocese. Although he was older than me, we had shared a great deal of our personal lives with each other, and having no family of his own, when he went on furlough to the UK, he often stayed with my family. I had not seen him for about six months since he lived across the Katsinala River about sixty miles away. With no phones and an unreliable mail service, arriving unannounced at a mission was very much the norm. We were delighted to see him. True to form, he dominated the conversation both before and after dinner. In addition to being a great raconteur, he gave us the latest news regarding the diocese and the Order.

Immediately after dinner, he invited me to take a walk with him alone.

"I would love to, Jack," I answered, "but you can see that a light rain has just started to fall. Let's go over to the church; there is lots of room there for us to stretch our legs."

"That's a great idea, Mike" he said. "The drive over here was long and bone crushing. I really do need some exercise."

The church was large, almost cavernous, and could hold over a thousand people, and we had it to ourselves. It felt comfortable chit-chatting with him, as we paced, side by side, up and down the long central aisle. I realized that I missed this sort of closeness. The moment, however, was short-lived.

"Mike, I have something very serious to discuss with you," Jack said, suddenly switching topics. "It's about your relationship with Sister Terry. It has recently been brought to my attention and I am afraid of you causing a scandal in the parish."

"What the heck are you talking about?" I asked in disbelief. "Are you joking?"

"Unfortunately, I am not. Your parents and family will be devastated if they discover that you are having an affair, and an affair with a nun at that. There is already talk all over the diocese about you."

We both stopped our pacing. I grabbed him by the elbow and stared into his face.

"Jack, you know me better than that. You know that it is not true."

"Unfortunately there is tangible evidence," he snapped back. "You have frequently been seen going off together, and I have a copy of a letter she has written to you."

Now I understood why he was visiting us. "Jack, I know where you've received your information from. It could only have come from one person. That bastard Les Turner gave you a copy of Sister Terry's letter."

"That's very unfair of you to say such a thing without any proof," he said, resuming his pacing. "Les is a fine priest and has the good of the diocese at heart."

"Les is an asshole," I barked back, my anger beginning to take hold. "You give him more credence because he is your classmate, because the two of you were ordained together. Is that the script here? Terry is my good and honest friend, Jack, and she has been very helpful to me as a counselor."

"Look, Mike," Jack countered, "counselors do not send love letters to the person they are helping. Counselors do not sign 'yours affectionately.' This clearly speaks to the kind of familiarity that should never exist between a priest and a nun. You need to tell me everything, and I will arrange to have you transferred to another parish. You can trust that I will do my best to contain the damage from this unsavory episode in your life. We have known each other for a long time; you can confide in me just how far this affair has gone, and what your intentions are."

"You are confusing agape love with romantic or erotic love. There is nothing else I can tell you," I replied, sitting down on the front pew, resting my head in my hands. My legs were feeling like jelly and pacing seemed like too much effort. "We are not sexually involved," I stated quietly. It was as if even using those words somehow sullied what was for me something treasured and very special.

There was a lengthy pause, with neither of us saying anything. He stood over me like a recalcitrant head master about to scold a disobedient student. "Are you telling me that there is nothing in this relationship that you would be ashamed to write home about to your sisters?"

Instead of keeping my composure and giving my defense, I decided I could take it no longer. "Don't you dare bring my family into this," I shouted jumping to my feet, "I'm not sleeping with her, Jack. Can't you understand," I shouted, "I'm not fucking her!" My loud cries reverberated and echoed off the tall bare walls. The church felt like a mausoleum and something inside of me was slowly dying. I felt dirty and unclean at even having to express myself in this way. But I had one last hope at convincing Jack.

"I have nothing more to say here, Jack. Why don't we go and discuss things with Andy?"

"I have already spoken with Andy about this," he announced knowingly, "but if you wish to do so, then let's talk with him."

Andy had just returned from doing his rounds at the clinic, so Jack asked if we could meet in the office. We rarely, if ever, used the office at night, and it felt strange and unfamiliar being there. Only one of the fluorescent lights was working; it had not been cleaned in years, and it cast a grimy, sepulchral pallor on the room.

"I have spoken with Mike about his affair with Sister Terry," Jack began, "and he denies any wrong doing. He says he has been open with you all along. So where do you stand?"

Just the way Jack presented the question, I intuited something was not right. There was a hesitation, before Andy finally spoke.

"I believed you Father Michael, and I trusted you," he began, not looking at me but directing his attention strangely to Jack. "But once I saw the letter and the note, I knew that my worst fears and suspicions had been realized. All of this time, the two of you have been living a lie, and have put the reputation of the mission at risk. What do you say to that?"

I could hear the steady beat of the generator coming from behind the kitchen. Somewhere near the market, a gun went off. The fruit bats dived and swooped rapidly in black swarms, and I could hear their distinctive high pitched squeaking as they landed and rustled together under the eaves of the house. Down the hallway, Nigel's radio was crackling, and I knew he was trying to catch the ten p.m. BBC World Service news. Through the open louver windows, the silhouette of our night watchman in his bright, yellow hat and raincoat was quite visible. He was carrying his glowing bush lamp and beginning to make his rounds. The rain made a gentle, soothing, consistent splashing sound as it ran off the metal roof onto the gravel below. Things appeared to be very normal, but the sense of betrayal I felt made it difficult for me to breathe. I had considered these men my brothers, but now that relationship would forever be flawed.

A calm and inward stillness crept over me. I loved just listening to the hypnotic music of the African night.

"I want no more part in this travesty of religious, missionary life," I said quietly, looking from one to the other. And choosing my words very carefully I announced, without wanting to make it too dramatic, "it has become a charade. I have some projects that I must finish in the next few weeks, but then, I will leave this diocese and Nigeria for good. I have no desire to discuss any issues with either of you any further. You have both betrayed me. I am innocent of your dirty accusations, and someday I hope to learn your motives."

The next two weeks were dreadful. The only person I could talk to was Nigel, and even he was nervous about getting too involved with my issues. When we were alone, he allowed me to vent and was, if nothing else, sympathetic. Each day was an emotional roller coaster as I struggled externally to complete my projects in the remote villages and hand over plans and schedules. Internally, I was trying to reconcile abandoning the work I truly loved, of helping people, something I had now been doing for ten years. I had never before really focused on the need to take care of myself. Now I realized that I was not leaving my job or my work: I was leaving my life. I would need to "let go" and let God show me a way that would let me continue to serve in His name, even without the formal structure of the Church.

Once word of my leaving was announced, there was a constant stream of people bringing me gifts and asking me to stay. Agabi, the headmaster, showed up one day after school, demanding officiously to see Andy. "If he is responsible for your going home, the parish has authorized me to take a delegation to the Bishop in Makurdi to have him removed. We want you to stay."

"No, Dennis," I begged, "there is no need to take such action. I have to go back to the UK to refresh myself."

"Then that is fine," he said. "I needed to hear it from your own mouth. We want you to come back to Adikpo when you return."

I thought about Terry constantly, and with deep affection for the help, support, and genuine friendship she had given me when I most needed it. Since she would not be back for another two months, I hoped that she would not be tainted by the sordid accusations. I decided to wait until I was back in the UK, and had more time and some distance from this community, to write to her in detail and let her know of my decision.

Lying in bed under my mosquito net just listening to the night, my restless mind would not let me sleep. I questioned the very fundamentals of my life — all of the long years of training and preparation; the joys and satisfaction of time spent ministering on my own in the 'bush' so close to the people; the physical and psychological demands, challenges and hardships, the lack of basic amenities; and especially, the aching loneliness. I knew no other work. I had never ministered in the UK. I had never served or helped white people. I had always wanted to be a Spiritan, always wanted to work in Africa, and now I was leaving them both. Would I do so permanently? Should I even leave the priesthood? Should I leave the Order which had promised me "brotherhood," but had only helped me find isolation, estrangement, and sadness? These thoughts scared me, and I tried desperately to think of something else.

I had arrived in Nigeria as a young inexperienced priest with the highest of ideals and aspirations. I was now leaving it as a mature seasoned missionary, profoundly disillusioned, and with so many deeply, personal questions unanswered. The words of an African proverb would haunt me for a long time to come: "He who questions, cannot avoid the answers." It was only now, that I was also beginning to understand the full meaning of what that schoolboy had said in my class in Keffi, so many years ago, "Slow slow, catch monkey," and the hunt had really only just begun.

EPILOGUE

My decision to move on with my life in a totally different direction only took place after much heartache and painful soul searching, a great deal of reflection and prayer, and tremendous stress.

After returning from Nigeria, feeling the need for a different kind of solitude and time to meditate, I entered a Trappist monastery in Northern Ireland, and became 'instant monk' for several months. From there, I spent a year living as a hermit. It was a wonderful, spiritually replenishing, and very special time. I was then assigned to work with young people in Scotland, especially helping recruit and develop future missionaries.

Puerto Rico was the last place I ministered as a priest. My Order asked me to be responsible for the training of future missionary priests, and to accept a position as rector of an international seminary in San Juan. All of my students came from Latin America. It was here that I finally came to the full realization that being a priest was, for me, like wearing a suit that did not quite fit. Externally I was obviously a good and successful priest. Internally, I was in crisis. I could no longer believe in my work. My theology was out of step with the mainstream Catholic Church, and as Rome began to silence theologians whom I considered to be on the cutting edge of serious thought, and slowly but persistently wind the clock back on the changes proposed by the Second Vatican Council, I knew I must move on. Loneliness had always been an issue for me, and I craved a real companion.

Three years after leaving Puerto Rico, I met and married a beautiful French lady in San Francisco, California. I obtained work as a social worker, and after completing a Ph.D. in Organizational Management became the Chief Executive Officer of a large healthcare corporation providing services to people with disabilities.

I am so grateful to have moved on with my life, and through my work with Rotary International I am still helping poor and marginalized people. As a volunteer Technical Advisor, I fly all over the world, wherever I am needed, trouble shooting and assisting with major humanitarian Rotary projects. I also started my own international consulting company, specializing in monitoring and evaluating humanitarian projects.

Memories of Nigeria: of people, their faces, parishes where I had worked hard and given some of the best years of my life, often flash before my eyes. There is some satisfaction knowing that perhaps I really have done some good. I know that in a very tangible way, I had changed the life of at least one person, Theresa Iyornumbe, by giving her my blood. I hope and pray that there are many others alive today, they and their families, who are still benefitting from my ministry and from that period of my life that I dedicated to them in a special way with all the commitment, energy, and idealism of a young missionary. As I continue my own professional and spiritual journey, enriched by my own life's experiences, those of others, and the opportunities that occur daily, I am at peace, knowing that in many ways I am still responding to the call I received many years ago to "change the world" though helping others.

ABOUT THE AUTHOR

Michael Barrington was born in Manchester, England, and was a member of a French Order of Catholic missionary priests. After working for ten years in Nigeria, he spent time in a Trappist monastery and later a year as a hermit. He lives in California with his French wife.